GOING ELEMENTAL

The Essentials of Success

Chris Richardson & Randall Gifford

SWAN JAGUAR PRESS | COLORADO SPRINGS

Published by Swan Jaguar Press
Colorado Springs, CO 80919
Printed in the United States of America
Copyright © 2015 by Chris Richardson & Randall Gifford
All Rights Reserved, Published 2015

Stories in this book have been altered to honor the privacy of individuals and organization referenced in the interview process, which are not directly connected to this body of work.

Going Elemental: The Essentials of Success | Chris Richardson & Randall Gifford. -- 1st ed.
ISBN 978-0-9961601-0-0
Library of Congress Control Number: 2015903489

Book Cover Design by Edie Everette
Illustrations by Edie Everette
Reference Tools by Chris Richardson & Randall Gifford
Editing by Sarah Davis & Nancy Fischman

To our children (Roman, Devon, Trevor, Cambria, Emma and Ian) and the future they deserve.

CONTENTS

ACKNOWLEDGEMENTS

Going Elemental is a creative collaboration of sixteen contributing authors, one amazing illustrator, and two very talented editors. Our deepest gratitude to Barbara Barrett, Bonny Stanley, Chris Guillot, Emily Stewart, Gordon Bonnyman, Janaki Severy, Julia Archer, Kani Comstock, Kenton Coe, Kirsten Smith, Lisa Fitzhugh, Mike Chitwood, Mindy Geisser, Rob Knauer, Nancy Fischman and Sarah Maclean Bicknell. Special thanks to Edie Everette for her brilliant illustrations, creativity and deep honoring of the stories shared. This book would not be possible without the tireless contribution, wisdom, creative guidance and support of our dear friend Sarah Davis.

ABOUT GOING ELEMENTAL

Going Elemental is a family of businesses with a mindset, method, and tools to help you see more choices in the way you inspire, lead, and achieve results. We go beyond outcomes to engage the whole person in mastering the elements of True Leadership using a system of success that's simply elemental.

Mindset

The elemental mindset requires self-examination, engaging in new ways of receiving information, and going beyond usual patterns of thinking and problem solving to generate new solutions. It's a practice of living in the question and allowing tensions to lead to creative discoveries that generate results.

Method

The **Going Elemental Method**™ **(GEM)** is an inside out approach to breakthrough innovation. The holistic method is used to create the transparency and visibility required to capitalize on every NOW moment.

You, the leader, are at the center of GEM™. As you apply our leadership practice in business and in life, you are creating change, success, and ultimately a permanent culture. Key components of GEM™ include:

- Create **Intent** that is realized through the development of a **Plan.**
- **Commit** with the full understanding of costs and risks, then **Resource.**
- **Empower** yourself to **Execute** on the specific actions with follow-up.
- Fully **Adopt** the outcomes to **Retain** the benefits over time.

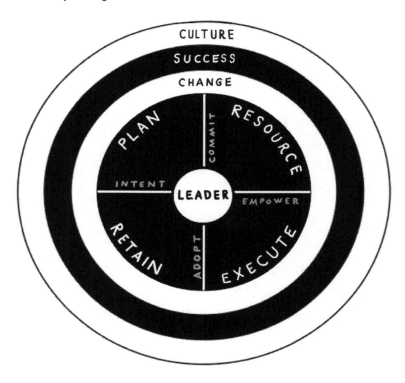

Tools

Our **Storytelling Framework**™ is a critical element of GEM™ and our development process. When we share our stories and reflect on the experiences we've had, we gain the wisdom to evolve past the limiting beliefs that hold us back. Our framework includes a personal interview, "I Am" poem, and the creation of a personal vision based on how you want to feel in all areas of your life.

The **StoryBoard Mapping Process**™ **(SMP)** is based on the key Elements of GEM™. Each Element has four components required for successful change at an individual and/or global organizational level. It is critical aspect of realizing results and sustaining success.

StoryBoard

INTENT plan	COMMIT resource	EMPOWER execute	ADOPT retain
VISION	RESOURCES	DESIGNS	SUCCESS FACTORS
PURPOSE	CAPABILITIES	ACTIVITIES	DEVELOP
CURRENT STATE	INNOVATE	PROCESS	BRAND
GROWTH	RISKS	APPROACH	COMMUNICATE

In our **Integrated People Strategy**, we develop a roadmap for attracting, developing, and retaining your most valuable asset - your people. We help you create a strategy with specific, actionable steps to support people in becoming the best at what they do. You walk away with an action plan and the tools for enabling high performance.

Family of Businesses

Going Elemental is growing individuals, teams and communities with a proven method of success developed over 25 years and used in every type of business from small start-ups to Fortune 50 companies. The foundation of our success in business is a critical part of our ability to develop True Leaders. Our companies include:

- **GEM Ventures**, an innovative firm specializing in business services, recruiting, and people strategies.
- **The Elemental Institute**, a center for Integrative Leadership providing executive development, mentorship, and business tools.
- **Evoke5,** connecting and developing the Going Elemental community through events, conferences, creative expression, purposeful travel, and reciprocity programs.

{1}

HOW IT ALL WORKS

Using the Going Elemental approach, we set out to explore the qualities of True Leaders. We interviewed people from all walks of life asking them to share personal and professional experiences of significant change and their definitions of success. Inspired by curiosity and a strong belief in the power of storytelling, we created a loose structure and a short list of questions, and engaged in a process of discovery. The results of this journey can be found in the pages of this book.

To help you navigate the Going Elemental concepts, we structured each chapter around a key Element of GEM™ (Intent, Commit, Empower, Adopt) and selected stories that best represented the sixteen components of the SMP™ tool (Intent: Vision, Purpose, Current State, Growth). We then looked for key themes across all the stories and highlighted examples of True Leadership. To bring this all together, we provided a sample story at the end of this section to model our approach.

We close the book with an invitation to discover your own unique way of moving through the world and how that informs your natural way of leading.

Key Takeaways

- Each of us has a unique way of moving through the world that influences how we lead. Aligning who we are, with what we do, and how we lead our life, informs our sense of success.
- Change is constant. How we perceive change plays a critical role in our quality of life. Learning to leverage change can dramatically accelerate our development.
- Owning our story is the beginning of living authentically. Being seen, heard, and open to feedback, gives us the wisdom to evolve beyond our own limiting beliefs.
- Feeling successful is a catalyst for rapid and sustained growth. Success is defined differently by each of us and is fertile ground for creative expression and celebration.

On True Leadership

This project expanded our idea of what it means to lead and enhanced our overall approach to leadership development. It had a powerful influence on our personal growth and validated our belief that we all have the capacity to be True Leaders in life.

True Leaders transcend the challenges and underlying forces of constant change. They experience, dream, collaborate, and risk. They create cultures that are alive, creative, adaptive, and resilient. They lead with intent and focus on sustainable solutions. They measure themselves by the path taken to achieve results and define success in terms of quality of life. They walk the talk, and in doing so, create a path for others to grow. Above all else, they create more leaders.

Our Process

Using the real life experiences of Going Elemental CEO Chris Richardson, we weave storytelling with our leadership framework, highlighting key references and Elements of GEM™ throughout her story.

Chris' Story

For some of us, there are specific events, or stuck places in life, that create an opening for a changed way of being. For me, that event came in the form of breaking my back in my early thirties. At the time it happened, nothing seemed out of balance because I busy powering through every aspect of my life. This experience showed me I was walking through life in a very inauthentic way, and I needed to change.

My story begins the day I fell over on the way to the bathroom. I didn't get up again for another four days. Despite my family's pleas to go the hospital, I simply lay in shock unable to feel the lower half of my body. My sense of control was paper thin, yet others were unable to influence a different outcome in this situation. The events of those few days spoke volumes about the true nature of my family dynamics. I drove everything, moved in ways I felt was correct, and rarely considered how to bring others along. All of the damage to my nerves, and the three years of recovery, could have been avoided had I not been so stubborn.

After several days, and with the help of narcotics, I finally moved from the living room to the operating room. After surgery, my doctor told me I needed to live differently if I didn't want to see him again. I had to come to terms with the fact I had been pushing through everything for so long that I stopped listening to others and the signs that my body was in trouble. I held tight to the idea that things were fine, when in reality they were not. I had been living inconsistently with who I really was, and it literally broke me. I now see the whole experience as a huge gift because it allowed me to see my life and my close relations in a different way.

I got real about the quality of my relationships and created a vision for my life based solely on how I wanted to feel.

I decided I would never go under the knife again, and with that INTENT everything changed. I made sure to COMMIT to a new way of living. Creating intention and keeping commitments to myself were important steps in becoming who I am today, but there was so much more involved. I needed to create ways to EMPOWER myself while making changes, and ADOPT practices that would allow me to continue to grow and evolve long after the crisis.

I promised myself I would start doing things I had never done before - things I enjoyed that would help my recovery. This included regular pedicures, ballet training, massages, and Pilates. After several years I was able to do Bikram Yoga, something I practice to this day. I was working in a job I did not enjoy, so I quit and started a family business. Creating space was important, so I took myself on weekly dates. Each week I would get in the car and start driving to destinations unknown. It was great fun, and helped me learn how to listen and respond to what I needed in the moment. Best of all, these commitments made it easy to say no to anything, or anyone, that didn't feed my sense of adventure or wellbeing.

Here is what surprised me. As I started to successfully remove the barriers and excuses that held me back, they were replaced with self-doubt, guilt, judgment, and resistance from others who had strong ideas of who I was as a person. My confidence was replaced with vulnerability, and for the first time, I was in a completely unfamiliar space. Being right was replaced with an endless supply of "I don't know." My need to stay busy was replaced with long periods of silence and sleep. My strong veneer was replaced with sensitivity and tears.

At times, it seemed easier to return to my old ways, rather than experience the discomfort of all these new and unfamiliar feelings. But I chose to stay the course for one important reason: I felt alive. The change I was experiencing was messy, uncomfortable, and at times very awkward, but it was real.

I began to see that my relationship with change was problematic and linked to experiences of pain, difficulty, or struggle. It's not that I ever resisted or feared change, but somehow my way of moving in the world resulted in me hitting a wall before I could see things in a new way. My back breaking was one form of hitting a wall.

I needed to break with the idea that change was painful and hard. So, I began to ask myself how I could do things differently and in ways I had not tried before.

Shifting my view of change transformed my life and my comfort level with the unknown. Ambiguity and uncertainty became a way of life and over time I began to thrive.

Prior to the experience of breaking my back, I had always put the needs of others ahead of my own. It was important for me to learn I could help my family if I focused on being the best version of myself. With the kids in particular, I wanted them to know that *life is choice, life is change and they alone influence the outcome of their own story.* So I started to align what I believed in and cared about with what I did. The continuity and consistency became evident to the people around me as I made new choices that set myself up for long-term success.

With the help of my partner in life, I became more of a parent, less of a friend, and created boundaries that never existed before.

Together, we made a series of new choices that supported the way I wanted to move in the world.

One of the best examples of leading significant change in the lives of others was when we began promoting a community mindset in running the household. The challenge was striking a balance between the demands of running our business and spending time as a family. After several experiments, we landed on a schedule where each of our six kids had full responsibility for the cooking and cleaning one day each week. We established clear ownership, put them in control of the menu and developed each of their individual talents. After almost two years in practice, the kids appreciate the work involved in maintaining a family, they take an active interest in what is being prepared, and they are grateful for the other days of the week when they can relax. Complaints about food and fighting over chores dropped dramatically, and we were able to create a balance that allowed for more quality time together.

> *It is critical to adopt practices that will help sustain change, monitor progress, develop skills, and ensure ongoing communication.*

Another example is related to creating change that supported how I was growing and evolving as a person. At one point, I hit a wall over going shopping with the kids because they would always make a play for something they wanted. The requests were endless, and it made it impossible to be fair to each of them individually. More importantly I didn't want to see them as entitled or spoiled, just because I was focused on releasing my attachment to material things. I became increasingly frustrated because how I was moving through life was inconsistent with all that surrounded me.

My partner and I came up with idea to have each child manage his or her own finances. This required some oversight and boundaries, so we created a process to review spending once a month to make sure all of the kids were being responsible and safe.

The point of the exercise was to help them appreciate the value of money and to learn what it's for—how it can be used, how it can serve, how it can hurt, how it can be wasted, and what happens when it runs out. All the children were given age appropriate budgets to buy their own clothes, pay for activities outside of school, and essentially manage their own decisions. The best we could do was counsel them on making good decisions, and work with them when they made poor ones. I remember many of our family and friends expressed concern over our decision, especially around the youngest and his capacity to manage his own finances at the age of 10. Boy, was I glad we stayed the course.

I am now a much happier mom. I am no longer inundated with the demands of others, or focused on everyone's use of money. To my surprise, the children started to change their behavior. Instead of buying new things, they negotiated to buy each other's used items. They started selling old items to build funds for things they really wanted. They started evaluating why they were playing sports, and what they really loved about those sports. Managing their own resources caused them to ask questions about what they wanted versus what they needed and could afford. They also became more generous souls, spending their money on each other in meaningful ways. And what was really fascinating was how their personalities were reflected in their management of money. We began to really understand what each of them valued and cared about in a way we had never considered before.

Now we know when the children make decisions, it's because it's important to them, and it's important for us to honor that. We still don't agree with everything they spend money on. But we are proud of the fact our children have life skills that are setting them up for success in the future. More importantly they have a sense of ownership of their own lives and their own decisions. Now they watch what we do and decide whether that resonates for them, creating a win-win situation for us all.

When we change and evolve in ways that feed us, we increase our capacity to parent, to lead others and to solve the problems facing our world today.

9

{2}

INTENT

Vision. Purpose. Current State. Growth.

Leverage the intersection of your dreams, vision, and aspirations with the current situation to move in the present with purpose.

Birth of Possibilities

VISION

When I was a young girl, I had a clear vision of how I wanted my life to be. I would be a research scientist, get married to a wonderful man, and have two children. I was a shy and rather introverted child, the good girl, despite my interest in science, which was unusual for a woman at that time.

I completed college, received my graduate degree, and married a wonderful man who was also a research scientist. By the time I was 26 years old, I was thrilled with where my life was. Then I had surgery and was told I could never have kids ... ever. Up to that point I had felt so unbelievably supported in all aspects of my vision, and then my vision was destroyed.

From the beginning of our relationship, my husband and I had talked about how many children we wanted and how we would raise them. Children were central to our life together. My husband realized that, for him, it was really important that they be his own biological kids—not adopted—though he was upset with himself that he felt that way. This was long before in-vitro fertilization. I felt damaged, worthless, and a burden. My body had failed me, and there was nothing I could do about it. I was depressed and felt so hopeless that I couldn't even talk to my husband about it anymore. I had this vision of being in a dark pit with steep walls that I couldn't climb up. My husband was in a different pit close by. We were trying to support each other, but we really couldn't connect.

I lost my interest in life and my passion for science. As a teenager I had saved my money for a microscope, and spent hours collecting specimens from nature and studying them. Now, I couldn't find anything to be interested in. I got so lost and desperate that I started thinking about suicide as a way out. It sounds stupid to me now, because I can't even imagine having felt that way. But then, it felt as if there were no options to get out of that pit. I started doing research on how to end the pain. Fortunately, after considering all the ways to kill myself, I found them not only unattractive, but also horrifying if they failed.

It was then that I realized I had to give up my plan for my life completely. I couldn't just modify the old vision that I had; I had to come up with a completely new one. I had to give it all up to survive and be alive again. When I made that decision, the world opened up and the lights came on in the darkness.

I convinced my husband that we should get a divorce so he could find someone and have his own kids. It was a hard sell, but I got him to agree. We spent a year after that decision doing things we had always talked about. We took a long trip to Asia, and bought things for each other. And then we went our separate ways.

I felt like I was a bird, flying free. Life was open to me; nothing was holding me back. I wasn't sure what I was going to do, but I had an idea that I wanted to work and live in Japan. I have had a fascination with Asia since I was five years old. Living and working in Japan was something I could get excited about. I left science behind, got a work visa, and began teaching English as a second language (ESL) at a school in Tokyo.

I was now in a completely different work environment and a different culture. I had never taught ESL, and I had no training except being an English speaker. I was one of a number of American and Canadian teachers in this fairly prestigious language school. Many of the teachers were looking at how to teach English to the Japanese in a different way. The way it was traditionally taught was so boring. Another teacher and I brought everyone together to discuss ways to improve the programs. We did a bit of research, collaborated with each other, created a proposal, and presented it to the president of this language school, who was also the school's owner. He was open to our proposal; so we were able to make changes in the curriculum, get new textbooks, and implement new ways of teaching. This was my first experience of creative collaboration to accomplish a goal.

Although the president agreed to the new system created by the teachers, the change was threatening to the director of the school. In Japan people often have jobs for life, but the director ended up quitting under the strain of the new system. The assistant director asked the president to promote me to be the director. I pointed out that I didn't read any Japanese, although I could speak some. If they wanted me to be the director, we would have to change the way the office was run. They were insistent that I assume the role. I accepted because they needed someone, and I had ideas.

In Japan generally, and in this school in particular, the men ran the offices and the women were receptionists who served tea. I gathered all the women together, and asked them if they were willing to step up and take on more responsibility. They were delighted. So I changed all of the receptionists into administrative assistants reporting to me, and as we worked together, we changed the way the whole school was run.

To lead as a collaborator is more creative

This was really fun for me. I loved that I got to change these women's lives. All the teachers were delighted, because we were able to do something fun. We had a whole new curriculum and textbooks. The students were happy. All of us got to contribute our creativity. For example, in speech class we gave the students the task of speaking about something in English that they could not share in Japanese. That opened them to a new dimension of language and was much more interesting to us as teachers. We introduced one of the very first homestay programs in Japan, which sent students to visit the United States for two weeks to stay with American families.

Once the president saw that my changes were having a positive effect, he let me make more. I think he realized that we were more creative than he was. We had a deal: I did all the negotiations, such as with the travel agents, and when he was asked what he thought, he would say, "I agree completely with the director." In my new position, I became a bold person. Moving out of marriage had been a very bold move for me. I became bolder and bolder with each new experience. The freedom of having nothing to lose allowed me to become the person who always speaks up when something isn't right. It has served me greatly. I am not a rabble-rouser, so I always do it from the perspective of what is valuable for the organization, not just for me. It is not about me. It is about the process, being on a team, collaborating.

When leading change in others, it's important to re-flect on what changed in one's self. All roads lead back to you.

The shy introvert disappeared. I was having a great time. We started having talent shows, dances, and other activities, transforming the school for both the students and the teachers. Originally when I went to Japan, I only planned to stay a year or two. I ended up staying for three years.

The experience in the school in Tokyo was the template for a lot of the things I have done professionally in my life since that time; collaboration, being bold, suggesting things when people say it can't be done. What happened in my personal life enabled these attributes. Having faced the idea of not being alive made being alive much more valuable. Why should I just spin my wheels or go along, when I see something that I feel could be changed for the better? I don't want to just go through the motions. I want to enjoy myself. I want to make a contribution and have value. I was willing to be the spokesperson.

For me, being forced to change my vision when I was young made me very bold. The sense of freedom I felt to do whatever I wanted was just huge. I already knew change was possible, because I had already changed my life. I felt the opportunity to make choices and not have to stick to them for the rest of my life—to actually be in the moment.

Feeling alive means enjoying what I'm doing, which is largely connected with creating and collaborating. There is vitality to creating. The creative process is like a drug. Creating is bringing something into existence that didn't exist before—a poem, a dinner, an organization, idea, book. That is exciting.

Creation is just being there in the moment. Of course, if you are going to create a building, that requires a detailed plan over months, but each moment contains the possibility of creation.

If you can get a group of people to be in the creative process together, amazing things can happen. The person leading the collaboration has to be open to other people's ideas. Then everyone has to be open to honing the ideas. The idea doesn't have to be 100 percent correct. It's all part of the process of creation. To bring about the moment of creation in relation to others, it is important to open the space for others to contribute. This requires us to be open to an idea that is not our own and to validate it when it shows up.

People need the freedom to be wrong or even completely right. They can't be afraid of making mistakes if they want to truly collaborate.

I think you have to experience collaboration to know that it's possible. If I were worried about always needing to be right about

19

everything, I would probably dictate versus collaborate. To collaborate, you have to be willing to be wrong.

The wisdom that comes from the creativity in a group is greater than one person's ideas. What do you have if you don't have collaboration? You have isolation.

One of the things I did when I came back from Japan was to create a new ESL center in the United States. Everyone on the faculty had experience teaching English to foreign students. We created the ideal program and it became a model for ESL learning in this country.

I started out as the director of the Hoffman Institute and expanded it internationally and then I became a teacher. I kept teaching because I can facilitate change in others. It is exciting to watch people blossom into their potential. I love teaching, because it is collaborative. Teaching the Hoffman Process is like an adventure.

I have had a lot of validation in my career, including running four organizations. Walking into any new organization, I want to remain open for input. When I am in a new situation I always start by considering what I can contribute. I am not a manager. I do not enjoy tending to the status quo. Creating is fun—bringing forth something that doesn't exist. If I don't have something to contribute, I move on.

A few months ago I was in Japan and spent time with two students of mine from the school in Tokyo decades ago and they talked about how much it changed their lives. I also spent time with one of the teachers and two of the women in the office who talked about what a big impact that experience had in their lives.

If you create an environment that is asking for creativity, collaboration, and honesty, then change happens.

I don't expect to make a big an impact in other people's lives. It is not about me. People have to change themselves. I can only offer opportunities. Some opportunities make it easier for people to change.

When I was young, I thought you planned your life and just went for it in a straight line. I remember there was a fellow graduate student who had his whole life mapped out on graph paper. We used to tease him, but maybe it was more common to have that kind of vision set out for your life so that you just kept going. Discomfort, trauma, or illnesses have a way of making us wake up to examine the options. I think if we get too comfortable with life, we won't necessarily be fully present or alive. The hard times in our lives teach us something: to look at life in a different way and that becomes a different blueprint for us.

I never imagined I would ever say this, but the decree of childlessness turned out to be a gift, a catalyst for change. I can imagine I would have modified my vision as I went through life, but without the shock I received and the ensuing depression, I cannot imagine I would have be able to split my life wide open. I realized then that I could change on a dime. There are immense possibilities. Life is not preordained.

I Am

I am surprised and delighted with the life I have created, so different than I envisioned.

I am a woman without children who thought they were critical for my happiness.

I am blessed that my mother guaranteed her daughters the same opportunities as her sons.

I am the child of parents who challenged me to live my dreams, however they unfolded.

I am the product of disappointments, personal challenges, and mostly good choices.

I am fascinated by the creativity, resilience, and resistance of the human mind.

I am guided by my spirit, amazed where it leads, and delighted in the mystery of life.

I am curious about life's possibilities and open to new perceptions and experiences.

I am passionate about whatever work I am doing.

I am in search of situations in which I can make a contribution.

I am a lover of travel that offers other perspectives on common human challenges.

I am an introvert who relishes authentic connection.

I am a writer who loves to get lost and found in the emerging words.

I am blessed with interesting colleagues, long-term friends, and siblings who delight me.

I am grateful to be alive, healthy, and living in a home and community I adore.

I am at my most relaxed in the tropics.

I am a learner, a teacher, a mentor, a coach, and a serious student of life.

I am eager to stretch my understanding of what is possible and what is real.

I am more bold and audacious than I imagined myself to be.

I am loved and loving and I love myself.

KANI COMSTOCK

Know Your Gift and Give It

PURPOSE

As a young child I was forced to take piano lessons. I hated performing, but I loved making the sound of music. When I was 13 years old, I came across some music paper and began putting down the notes I was playing. The experience of writing music thrilled me; I never stopped after that.

If you enjoy what you're doing and it is not harming anyone else, you should follow it because you won't be happy otherwise. This is the life I want to live. It is a combination of undying interest in a certain subject and a willingness to pursue it above all else. At my age, looking back at my life, I have few or no regrets.

Persistence and a huge amount of luck have allowed me to continue working at something I love for the past 60 years. I always tell kids who ask me about composing to keep a low overhead, so you can go through doors when they open. I am a believer in doors opening.

When I was in college, planning to get a degree in the history of music, I had an experience that changed my entire life. I discovered that Nadia Boulanger was still teaching summer classes at Fontainebleau, outside of Paris. Nadia was such an austere woman, and famous to so many American musicians of that time. Many respected composers studied with her in the 1930s and '40s. I thought it would be a wonderful experience to spend two months studying with Nadia, so my Godmother arranged the finances to go to Europe as a gift for my graduation. I studied with Nadia for two months. During my last lesson that first summer with her, she asked me to stay and continue my studies.

She said she thought I had talent. No one had ever told me that before. It thrilled me that someone would affirm and support something that I wanted to do. I told her I couldn't afford to stay, and she told me to go back to Tennessee, get prepared, and come back. Then she arranged all the scholarships to cover my expenses for three years. A wonderful French family "adopted" me. After studying with Nadia, I was able to get a job in Paris. Since then, my life has been jumping from one extraordinary experience to another.

Often there is a moment when someone sees something in another person, which can change everything.

It makes me sad to recognize that so many gifted people don't have the kind of opportunity I had. I believe sometimes people have to go far from their roots to find that. I gave a college commencement speech recently encouraging the students to travel, get out of their towns, and relate to others around the world. I believe everyone has a gift for something. I once filled in for a local music teacher in an elementary school. There was an eight-year-old child who had perfect pitch and an amazing talent for music. I went to his parents and told them that their child had a special gift. They did not show any interest in pursuing or encouraging it. I have no idea what ever happened to him.

As a member of an arts council, I encourage people to invest in kids with talent using their resources to change these kids' lives. It has been challenging to find the right approach to encourage people to support talented kids to find their path. It brings me pleasure to try, though I don't always succeed. Patrons of the arts see the talent in a young person and help it be realized. When I am trying to raise money for an art project, it is important that the would-be patrons see the results of their investment and take joy in it.

It is a gift to be able to help change the lives of others.

When I left Paris for New York as a young man, I was passionate about writing my first opera. I thought that if I could write an opera, it would propel me into the spotlight of the music world. Anyone who sits down to write an opera should think twice, because they are so expensive to produce. The chances of a production are near zero. It was naive to think I could get a new opera performed, but I knew the only way to be sure it was not performed was if I didn't write it! I wrote the opera based on a famous French play, *South,* by Julien Green. The Opera of Marseilles picked it up, which was an amazing phenomenon. Luck and the help of friends pushed it along. The first time I heard any of my work played professionally was during rehearsals. When I was asked what I thought after the first hour of rehearsals, I told them I thought it was incredible. After having spent so much time and effort writing it, listening to the music, even badly played, was beautiful.

Success, for a musician, is just survival, but I have been able to successfully work as an independent composer my entire life. I have a large network of devoted friends who encourage and support me, and I feel that is what life is all about. We are all in an eternal struggle and we have to help each other through it. Many years ago I wrote the musical score for a French movie produced by an American studio, and I thought it would be my ticket to the big time. The movie was never produced due to a federal lawsuit that broke up the industry monopoly at the time. In retrospect, I would probably have succumbed to the underside of Hollywood and died young! I realize that I am where I should be in life, and I am grateful to be able to say that.

I know people who regret things that have happened to them or choices they made, but it is because they didn't change with the opportunities. Everything changes all the time. You know that winter will eventually come, and you prepare by getting a warm coat. Recognizing change in others, and dealing with that, is more complicated. For me, there are two aspects of happiness. The first is being happy in a given moment or happy in reflection of a moment that has passed. The second is the happiness of the soul that one feels when one is creating. There is a mental state you go into that takes you away from worldly troubles.

The struggles of the world are offset by the personal experience of creating.

Everyone has the capacity to create something—happiness for others, helping others to be free from pain. There are so many ways someone could be creative. It is not limited to the "Arts." But I believe art is a part of life and should be integrated into a practical existence.

People are curious about creative musicians. I compose because of the impact it has on other people. I wrote a piece for a PBS documentary film, *To Render A Life*. I gave a CD of the music to a friend in the Midwest. She wrote me a letter telling me that she had a friend dying of cancer in the hospital. Every day, over a period of some weeks, her friend would ask to have this piece played for her. The music had created a connection with her soul. It was something that brought her pleasure and peace until the moment she died. That is the highest compliment and reward that I could be given, a reward beyond all financial consideration. Creative people often ask themselves if their work is worthwhile. This experience made me feel that what I had been doing is not a loss.

I believe we are all on a path to somewhere; we are put here to do something on this earth.

If you are aware of what your talents are, you will follow that path, and change will help you realize it, for better or worse. I think everyone has opportunities and, if we recognize the signs, we can make the right choices.

I Am

I am at the top of a hill with a view onto the long, long road that put me here.

I am playing solitaire and hoping that each move will find the cards in a winning order.

I am aware that cards do not always cooperate, but when they do, I am thrilled; and when they don't, I am certain the next deal will work.

I am content to have this view of that long, long road, and more conscious now of the twists and turns that I took.

I am seeing more clearly the lessons I was taught along the way, and I am not disappointed that normal eyesight weakens.

I am certain that inner sight is strengthened as outer sight diminishes.

I am looking forward to the next deal of the cards.

KENTON COE

Live in the Question

CURRENT STATE

The early deaths of my immediate family caused me to shift how I saw the world and to redefine the meaning of life. My father died in a car accident when I was 15. My younger brother died of hepatitis and pneumonia when I was 21, and my mother died suddenly in less than 24 hours when I was 26.

Walking through these losses brought challenges and gifts I could not have imagined. They invited me to look beyond my childish belief that those we love will live forever and, instead, invited me to stand directly in the truth that physical life is short and precious. I think of my journey in terms of three openings. Each death invited me to search for a reality far beyond a single lifetime. When I was young, I felt life was a mystery full of Angels and Spiritual Beings who watched over us. Both of my parents believed in God and held strong Protestant values, although they were not churchgoers. I knew there was a magnificent Being who loved us and would respond to my prayers, and I attended different churches every Sunday with various neighbors. This church hopping may have set the stage for my spiritual rather than religious stance now.

My dad was a dentist and a scientist, and we spent hours talking about the magic of the human body and exploring the *Encyclopedia Britannica,* trying to understand the universe, volcanoes, plants, and obscure nuggets of knowledge. In today's world, my dad would be identified as a high functioning person with Attention Deficit Hyperactive Disorder (ADHD). He would watch TV, listen to his transistor radio with an earplug, and read a book, all at the same time, and he could track all three. He taught me to wonder about things and ask questions.

My mother was very social. She grew up as a Florida debutant in a small town and was schooled in the art of etiquette. She was artistic and made Japanese flower arrangements and dressed in very unique and classic styles, loved to dance and embroider, and was always making wonderful magical things for the house. She was an avid reader and was fascinated by the human spirit. She would cook with precision and make the most beautiful things to eat. She taught me compassion and care giving.

I loved both parents with all my heart. Unfortunately, somewhere along the line, they fell out of love with each other. It is hard to say if drinking led to their discord, or if their discord led to their drinking, but both of them became periodic alcoholics. They drank very heavily on the weekends, and this often led to horrific verbal assaults of one another. I knew my parents loved me and were good people, yet they were angry, unhappy, and clearly unable to manage their differences. I often wrote to God to ask for help and to give us all some kind of peace.

When confronted with challenges, how we see the world shifts.

When I was 14 years old, they could no longer live together, so my dad moved out and into an apartment. A few months after he left, we learned that my dad had been having a relationship with a female family friend. He eventually married her. My mom felt angry, betrayed, and attacked him on every visit. As a result he made fewer visits, and at some point I barely saw him. Less than a year later he died in the car accident. When dad died, his widow reached out to me and some years later shared that he stopped visiting because he felt the fights were damaging. She ultimately became a mother figure to me, because I was willing to change how I saw things.

I was devastated when Dad died. I stayed home from school that week, reading the Bible and writing in my diary. I began to ask questions: was my dad completely gone or was it just his physical being? What is life? What is death? What is the energy of the life we see and feel? Does it exist in memory, a photograph, in a word or song? How do we hold that existence inside us and keep it safe?

On my way back to school that Friday, I learned that President Kennedy had been shot. The world was in shock and abject fear for our country's future. Both the president and my dad were 42 years old when they died. I went to school to talk to people about how hard it was to lose my dad, and everyone was focused on the president being shot. I thought my friends would be consoling me, yet I began comforting my classmates and helping them in their grief. The whole country was completely derailed, asking, "Why did this happen?" and, "Now what do we do?" I had just been asking myself those same questions. Kennedy was the "father" of our country, and his death threw people into a place of confusion and fear. I had come back to school having dealt with the same confusion and fear. I saw how transient life was and understood we could leave at any moment for any reason.

Life is precious. We must make it wonderful.

After my father's death, being home was very painful. My mother's drinking escalated, and much of her anger and grief was directed towards me. I became cautious, not wanting to trigger an attack. Meanwhile, I was struggling to reconcile my love for my dad and my anger at the man who left my mother and me.

For my brother, the experience was devastating. He began using drugs, got in trouble often, and did poorly in school. I felt so helpless as I watched him struggle. He was such a beautiful soul. He gave to everyone and was very loved. When his friends decided to join the military, he quit high school and enlisted in the Army. The recruiter told my brother to lie about being in trouble with the police so he did not disclose having stolen a motorcycle as a minor.

The military gave my brother the structure he needed. He began to flourish and receive awards for successes. Then one of his platoon members got caught smoking marijuana. They ran special screening on everyone and found out he had lied about the theft, and he was dishonorably discharged. When he came home his spirit was crushed. My mom signed him up for community college to learn a trade, but he rarely attended.

One day he came to my mom's apartment very sick and barely able to stand. He had contracted hepatitis and needed to be hospitalized. Within a few days he contracted pneumonia and died at age 19. He was the dearest of souls and my baby brother. Once again I was given the opportunity to honor the passing of a family member. I held a wake for him, and we all mourned the loss of his beautiful and unfulfilled life. For his funeral, the girls got their hair done and wore their best clothes. The boys wore slacks and jackets. His death woke them up and caused them to take a look at their choices.

For the next five years I studied everything I could find in metaphysics and spiritual studies to help me understand life and death. Then one night I received a call that my mother was in the emergency room, and within 24 hours she was dead at age 54 from ruptured organs that had poisoned her heart. After mom died, I began to have premonitions. I thought that I would die in a car accident by the age of 54. I wasn't afraid of dying, but I was sure I would not live long, so I never planned for the future. I didn't save money or think about retirement. I was living my life fully, and I felt that if I died tomorrow, I would have no regrets. It was more surprising that it didn't happen as expected.

The deaths in my life at an early age were a big surprise. I began to look for ways to integrate the unknown through meditation and study of yoga. I often draw on two quotes from my beloved yoga teacher. One is *"Be 100 percent planned and 50 percent flexible."* The second is *"Don't make appointments in life so you won't be disappointed."*

Just about the time that I think I have a handle on life I experience another unexpected turn of events. Then I ask myself questions like how can I see it differently, what can I learn from it, and what is the opportunity? With questions as my guide, I have become skillful at changing how I see things so that I do not get stuck or feel trapped.

the
nature
of
change
is
to

unlearn
and
relearn
constantly

I fall in love with every person I meet. That includes the high school kids I worked with for 16 years who had emotional problems. Most people misunderstood them and feared them. Yet, when I read their files I realized that due to their emotional issues these youth were often abused and harmed by their own families, which made things worse. Therefore, I loved them because of their willingness to take on life. They had the courage to want a better life and be angry, not apathetic. I believe people naturally want to be more, to be better, to be understood, to be heard. The angriest person is trying to be more heard, more appreciated, more seen.

In order to have compassion and forgiveness, we must first love ourselves so we can love and forgive others.

My work now is in the area of training and development, performance improvement, coaching, and facilitation. When I am working on improving the performance of an employee, I start by asking the boss if she really wants to keep the employee. If she says "No," I ask if she has told her employee what needs to change for him to succeed. I tell the boss that if I am just a stopgap prior to firing this person, don't hire me. Then I ask if the person does change, is the organization going to be able to see him in a new way? I influence change by holding people accountable for their seeing. I believe we see what we believe is true. If you believe your boss is out to get you, you'll assume his or her actions are focused on getting rid of you, whether that is the truth or not.

My gift is to connect with what is underneath the layer we see. I communicate with a person's spirit, their soul. I see beyond the words spoken.

For some of us there is a unique connection that is underneath the obvious. If we don't listen, we miss it.

I always ask the same questions; Who are you? What is important to you? What is your life like? Can I help you? The questions are the vehicle through which I can connect. We all have an opportunity to listen differently, contextually, at the soul level. When we do, people show up in a very different way.

It is so much more powerful to be curious than to be right.

Deep down the important question is: are we alone or are we connected? We know we are connected to our close friends. Usually, if a close friend tells us we have caused them pain, we listen, and we are willing to change to create a mutually beneficial relationship. When we experience ourselves as part of a continuous web of connections, we have an ability to understand the perspective of other people.

It's more powerful to ask respectful questions than to assume the answers. If we can listen differently, the world will be more connected with fewer barriers. When you find yourself living in opposition to what your heart wants you to do, ask questions that will help you get back on track. There is a rhythm in the universe, and we need to be open to that. When a humpback whale starts singing a different song, soon the whole pod is singing a different song. Life itself is a dynamic process. Change is constant and I saw how fragile life was. The question is how can I partner with the change? When life is overwhelming, how do I protect myself?

Each of us has a different capacity to change. It is important that we partner to help each other in change. For example, in 1965, schools taught students there were only a few right answers and they could memorize them all. Today, we teach that the world is constantly providing new answers and we cannot stay current. We do not teach final solutions, instead we teach how to learn, integrate, and apply new learning. The conversation has shifted from final outcomes to process mastery.

Human beings are creatures of habit. The brain memorizes things so it doesn't have to work as hard. Those memories become patterns. Then you realize that what you learned no longer works for you or you understand it is simply no longer true. So you have to break all those patterns. We naturally think in outcomes, always looking for the answer, but there isn't a final answer. Life is about the quality of the journey we are on. It is a continuum: evolving, ever-interesting, and always surprising.

I Am

I am the sun, the moon, and the stars

I am the earth, the wind, the sky, and the sea

I am that which was created

I am that which is from the created

I am blessed to be part of all.

I am humbled by the all that exists

I am grateful to be an eternal Spirit

I am honored to see Oneness every day

I am aligned in my Soul to truth

I am called to see, feel, and express that truth.

I am at peace knowing I sleep in a conscious Universe

I am told to teach others how to feel Unity

I am compelled to live that which I teach

I am the flame, the candle, and the light

I am an expression of peace and eternal love for all.

JANAKI SEVERY

See It. Be It. Do It.

GROWTH

Ceremony has changed me completely. It has brought my inside out, where everyone can see it. It has brought out my confidence and sense of self beyond anything I could have imagined. I have been doing ceremony for 25 years. I am now able to lead it at the same time I am going through it. Who I am today is totally due to ceremony.

I have been drawn to ceremony since I was a child. Friends and I would dress up as jesters and take our show on a cart into town, totally lost in the characters. After that I was involved in theatre, performing at a very young age. Theatre was my life until I was 32. I choreographed, created, and put companies together. That gave me a strong understanding of how things are put together in the physical world. The stronger you can see in your imagination, the stronger the results on the outside. I gathered a lot of information without even knowing why I was gathering it. Later, when I went into spiritual practice, it felt very familiar. My strong imagination makes me comfortable with all sorts of spiritual activities. Inside the imagination, I have always known myself. It is that joyful place, a place of being alive.

I am committed to putting as much life back into the world as I can, to create beautiful energy here physically, by developing a path of kindness and compassion that is constantly growing. First,

45

you have to start with kindness and compassion towards yourself. For me, this came as a result of my daughter's death. We live in a culture where we expect to die before our children, unlike cultures in other parts of the world where this type of loss is commonplace. I lost my parents and I reevaluated my life and values, but my experience after the loss of my daughter was far more traumatic. It turned my world upside-down. Based on my daughter's death, I made some very new agreements with myself about how I live in the world. It was time to live inside out.

Her death was the catalyst that made my "outer" my "inner." I couldn't find myself. I didn't understand why I had to be taken to that low point. The moment of death is sacred and you come back changed. You go through amazing guilt: why didn't I spend more time with her? What did I do to cause this? You go through an internal cleansing. However, I made that awful experience good, and that is very characteristic of me. My cosmology accepts what happens, and asks how I can move from there, and how can I heal myself and help others. Both her birth and her passing were somewhat bookends in profoundly altering the course of my life.

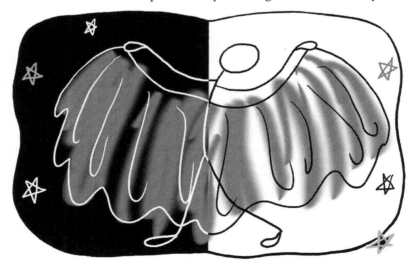

I was born into a family that would have put me on a track with a predictable outcome, but I went off the track when I was pregnant at 15. My parents would support me in whatever choice I made, which included getting married and having my daughter. Much later, I asked myself why I had gotten pregnant and married at 16. I realized that I was trying to live a fairy tale. I had been raped at 14, and subconsciously, there was a craving in me to put something right that had felt wrong and hurtful. I was raised with romantic ideals, and I was looking for Prince Charming.

Having a baby, getting a job, and figuring it all out were big circumstances where I had to put aside a lot of teenage activities and grow up fast. I always say that my daughter saved me from becoming an alcoholic, or drug addict. Having her protected me through what was a precarious time for many people. More importantly, I knew this new soul, her soul, needed to come forward into life.

My husband and I were very much in love with each other, but as is often the case with teenagers, it didn't last long. By the time our daughter was three, we were in the middle of a divorce. I had a new boyfriend, and was working professionally as a choreographer and dancer/performer in the West End of London. I was 19 then, and my mother suggested that I go to America to help my sister, who had just adopted my two nephews and found out she was pregnant with a third child. My parents offered to pay my way to Pullman, Washington. I didn't want to separate from my boyfriend, I had good work and a house in London, but intuitively I knew the trip to America was the right move. I have been here in America ever since.

In the mid to late 1980s, I experienced a shattering crisis of faith. This led me to change tracks from theatre and dance to follow the path of spirit and sacred ceremony. This looked more different on the outside. Inside it felt like I was continuing the dance that I have always expressed. I was deepening and deeply connecting. In this place of fully living, I awoke to how I had become disconnected. It was then that I took myself into the indigenous cultures to bring greater depth, and meaning, and understanding of ceremony and healing for myself. And then, like so many, I wanted to share the value with others. Out of a previously more artificial sense, I was now moving to root it in relationship and connection to life.

Ceremony is not ritual; ceremony is enlightened change.

Ceremony for me begins with calling the directions—the four cardinal points and the above and below. This sets sacred space and prepares me for spiritual practice and healing. The way I call the directions, just by myself, for myself, I would call a ritual: a repeated action and pattern recognized by the invisibles, "Oh, she needs sacred space." After I have done that, I sit alone and wait until I feel a transformative feeling about a situation or what I could do differently. This is my personal work. Once I realize what my shared memory is with the event or person (what part I am responsible for) I become informed as to what needs clearing or cleansing, then I pray.

When I call in the directions with community, that is a part of a ceremony. Ceremony engages the whole community within sacred space and focuses a sense of oneself in each individual. It accesses the ancient wisdom of understanding to create change in your life, to celebrate and experience gratitude. Those dynamics can create good into the world that changes people. It's about being connected with a community of likeminded people and generating incredible energy. The whole of life is happening there.

I was carrying masks, not representing who I really was, when I experienced true ceremony for the first time. Ceremony connected to who I am inside, showing me and calling me to remember what I was really about. Visions then started coming in very doable ways. Today my "inner" leads me through the world and is who I am. My trainings with Native Americans continue to keep shifting my awareness and understanding, and this moves me into my next growing edges.

Ceremony is alive, functioning, and engaging. The more I do it, the more my true inside nature of joy comes out. People may not have been able to see this inner me until the last 15 years or so. As it emerged, I was amazed at the backlash around me; people who were invested in me being not seen—an old way of seeing me that was more about the old masks. I held firm in my vision. Then it started to manifest on the outside. There was a lot of antagonism and criticism toward me while this was happening.

I realize now, that is a natural way of breaking the surface. Now when people come to me with a vision trying to manifest and they are experiencing all the barriers that I did, I can empathize with all the resistance from their outside lives. People get used to seeing you in a certain light, in a certain role—it's an illusion you have created between you and them. You have to shatter those illusions. You have changed. It has huge backlash.

At a certain point I had to leave my extended family. I can't stop who I am just because they can't experience the changing me. Now, years later, I can go back, and there is a place of more understanding. I never gave up my faith, belief, confidence, and vision in myself. I knew myself differently this time; I was better, stronger, and very connected. Now when I help people, I look for those crucial points that generated change for me, and I now witness in others.

The lack of self-love in individuals is the greatest cause of the suffering and pain in the world.

Fundamental to me is the ability to turn negative situations into integrity and coherence. Sometimes it takes me a long time to recognize a negative situation but once I do recognize it, I turn it into something of value. People sense that when I am working with them. Even if they don't know my story or they haven't had the same experiences, they know the words I am speaking are coming from a place of empathy instead of sympathy. When people come to me, there is a resonance: my subconscious is talking to your subconscious. There is a sense that I have had a lifetime of traumatic experiences and can therefore relate that wisdom. Through empathy, I facilitate a discussion between you and yourself.

When you grow in self-love, in the very core being of who you are and being part of the whole picture, then you begin to grow real self-confidence, direction, and purpose inside of yourself, and then change organically and naturally occurs. The more you grow, the more you become who you are right now as a contributing and essentially valuable human being. It starts with knowing yourself.

The best way to impact change in other people is to see it, be it, do it.

Everyone has a sense of himself or herself, as a being of loving capacity and generosity. It is that so many layers of generational misunderstandings, defensive memories, and dead end beliefs cover us. It has been so important for me to connect to my essential self. I needed to get in touch with my sense of my eternal nature. The "me" goes way beyond this present experience of inhabiting this body called "Sarah." I have found that if you continue to set your intentions and clear your environment to support your emergence, you will change. Step by step, you grow.

Change takes time. The only change that is worthwhile for me is organic. Change evolves our way of thinking and seeing differently. I need to be willing to experiment to find the change

51

that I want. You or I can also mentor change in others, if you're just a little farther down the road than that other person. Honesty and discipline are what has worked for me.

Doing this creates an energetic exchange with people. A larger presence is felt. The way I live my life, hopefully, allows presence to take residence. The best way to impact change in our families, in communities of work, and friends appears to be by showing presence and by acting outwardly from that greater awareness of life—a life where human potential informs and brings goodness into the room. This helps me choose kindness and compassion and means I do not hold myself apart from you or my own experiences or traumas. We are both seen in the room.

SOMETIMES THE RIGHT THING TO DO IS WAY BIGGER THAN OURSELVES

It's important to look at a situation and choose the most illuminated option—the option where everyone gains. This is how I make decisions. I try to make sure that my actions cause no hurt or harm to others. And this is how we care for each other as a family and community.

When you speak, you are manifesting. You need to feed the core self, rather than focusing on how you are perceived. Once you focus on your core self, all the rest fades away. Stay with the core of who you know yourself to be. Stick with that core sense of knowing, and it will work out.

For me, change only happened because of a very significant catalyst, because I was so strong-headed. There was a lot the world had to teach me. My cosmology suggests a lot of chaos before a new sense can emerge. I had to go down the drain to know I didn't want to do that again.

I Am

I am born of Mari, born of Alice Maclean born out of the west highlands of Scotland, of Gaelic language and Queen Victoria's empire.

I am born out of the British Empire, of Shanghai banks, of whaling, and Newcastle beer.

Born out of Clarence Bicknell, Esperanto, and wild alpine flowers, out of Constable and knights and those who burnt King Alfred's cakes.

I am born out of stone and wild moorlands, of moss and the fae who travelled west through the Summer Isles on an immram of her own.

I am a Brit who washed up on the shores off the Pacific Northwest amidst seaweed, ravens, and cedar bough; who found her feet amidst clabber board, wild mountains, and cranberry bogs.

I am a person who loves and changes and creates as she goes.

For I am many lifetimes all rolled into one, a traveller, a juggler, anam cara, and priestess.

I am one who has been adopted by these shores, who stands in immigration lines and clutches a green card.

I am she who found her place inside and out at the feet of Native wisdom borrowed and returned.

I am the medicine of my rowan roots interwoven with wild salmon and Douglas fir.

I am Grandmother Turtle landing in meadowland, fresh from the ocean currents of life.

I am earth person, vulnerable to the song of life, and I follow my breath.

I am she who crosses oceans and cultures to connect and be whole, one who dances with others in shared language of the soul.

I am a dreamer, a sharer of truth, an assistant, a collaborator.

I am a special education teacher, a mentor of life, a student, and a poet.

I am a lover, a wife, a mother, a ceremonialist, and shadow doctor of grace.

I am you, I am me, and I am continuing our prayer to love even more, to be kind even more, and be here even more, whomever we be.

Sarah Maclean Bicknell

{3}

COMMIT

Resources. Capabilities. Innovate. Risks.

Spend your time and money resourcing your vision creatively, considering all possible scenarios and risks for achieving your objectives.

Back Your Dreams

RESOURCES

What I carry around with me are memories of childhood, when each day held the magic of discovering the world. Sometimes that magic has been forgotten. We might wonder how to find the little path that will lead us back to ourselves. This is my story of finding that little path.

Children discover the world in various ways. For me, the outdoors was my world, a world that nurtured the wild child in me. I played beneath trees and shrubs, and climbed maples, mimosas, and elms. I built a circle of stones underneath the shrubs near the side porch of the house where I lived. My sacred place, my hidden retreat was that circle of stones. I made many places like that in my yard. I collected items to adorn the spaces and I buried secret messages and dreams in tiny aspirin tins to be opened when I was older; I thought 15 years sounded about right. Except that by then, I had forgotten those sacred places and where the tins were buried, and even what my dreams written on scraps of paper inside those tins had been.

Where does change begin? End? Start over? Cross over? What is living in change? Where are the punctuations of change? How do we understand its meaning? These are the questions I ask myself today, as a result of this interview. The unexpected consequence was that the questions led me back to my childhood. So I will pick up my story from inside my stone circle near the porch.

One crisp autumn morning when I was about seven, I was making a volcano of crunchy brown leaves in the front yard. I ran against the breeze, leapt and dived, my splayed body landing right into the middle. Muffin, our black cocker spaniel, dashed around the leaf pile tugging at the bottom of my jeans. I lay in the hole of my making, surrounded by the leaves, turning to face the sky.

"Leaf girl," I thought.

Suddenly I heard the squeal of tires and shouting. Prying myself from the leaves, I hurried towards where the sound of the tires had been. From the top of the driveway, I looked down and saw the milkman's truck around the big willow, its rear tires embedded in the ditch. Mother was sitting on the hard driveway just behind the truck, cradling Muffin.

Even now, that scene is burned in my memory. I saw, I felt, I ached. I felt the pain and suffering of the Other, and in the heart of the Others. I felt keen awareness of my own little place on earth, and of the things that change quickly and unexpectedly. I knew in that moment there was nothing I could do about them, ever.

I have thought about the deaths of my parents. My father died after a brief illness, but at the time my perception was that he was getting better. I clearly was in denial that his continuous weight loss was precipitating his death. I was 32 years old and had started graduate school. After his death, I felt I couldn't muster the strength to finish my classes that semester. But I managed. Mother was there.

I can see that change takes someone believing in you, or you believing in yourself. I had a friend who really believed and had confidence in me and saw something in me. She worked for a statewide organization and she asked me to take a leadership position in a large local non-profit. I took it mostly because she believed in me, and I thought I would like to make a difference, but secretly I thought that if the work got too difficult (because it was a dysfunctional organization), I could just leave.

It was a lot worse than I thought: the organization was on the brink of closing down. Literally, on my second day in the office, things began to flow. The pipes had burst and a full force of gushing of water had flooded the storage room where all the boxes containing years of paperwork were stored. A couple weeks later a wonderful older woman walked through the door. She had been a corporate executive secretary, and she was looking for a part-time job. She helped me reorganize everything. We cleared the clutter of the organization and reestablished trust with the community.

People understood we were a sick organization so we had to change. I engaged a lot of people with creativity and inspiration and made sure everyone had a voice. It was difficult and took a long while. I dismantled the entire board of directors, started from scratch, and lit new fires. We were a phoenix rising from the ashes.

Live on the edge, take a risk, and join in on the adventure.

This experience gave me a lot of confidence. It began with my being seen. After that, I developed a better ability to see other people myself and to reflect to them their possibilities. This affirmed the power of what happens when you are open to new possibilities and can move fearlessly through open doors.

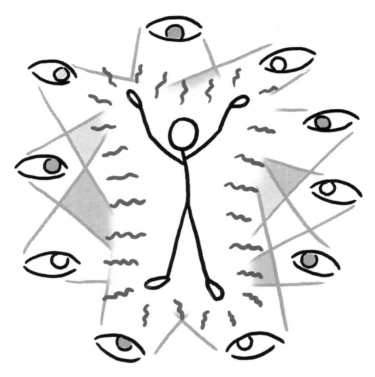

Often you find what you love to do by finding people who you love to be around. Together you explore, play, laugh, create, and find moments of serendipity.

In my experience you have to keep open the doors because that's your potential for change. There may be a time within a system, an organization, when there is too much sameness. Even though I felt I empowered the organization where I worked with creativity, newness, and freshness, and it had evolved for a period of time, there came a point when it stopped feeding me in return. It was time to leave.

Now I am in the best place of my life where I feel a greater motivation, power, flexibility, and agility in all that I do. And all that I am doing seems to have greater significance than ever.

My awareness opened more as I grew up. I think I changed by degrees. First, I learned to recognize opportunities presented in my life. And second, I learned to be more fluid, to accept and walk through the doors that were opened for me. This is a choice.

My childhood circle of stones was a solid area of protection. Stepping out of it and out of my childhood, I imagine now that this circle pulsates, that it is one of movement flowing in and out, approach and retreat, always moving and never static. It spirals and it showers transparent sweetness. Its breath creates new stories. How the stories are interpreted will either put a heavy rock in the circle or a ray of sun. It's a choice.

Wherever you are, love all that you can. When you see another, see something of their potential, because that is also within you.

I honor my parents because they were the first influence on me. They defined and shaped me with the best of intentions and gave me the space to create my circle of stones and then step out of it. As you look outside your circle it is important to recognize the invitations to step over the edge, because they may not be very obvious. And keep finding the edge, because that is where your best place is. I'm on the journey, too.

I Am

I am a child of the Appalachian Mountains in East Tennessee.

My family from Scotland, Ireland, England, and Wales settled in these hills and hollers, making the best of a hardscrabble life.

I am a small miracle—an only child born to older parents. I was encouraged but not spoiled; loved but not indulged.

I was a wild child, outdoors with my dog, friends, and imagination—"The Greatest Show on Earth!"—a trapeze artist on my swing set, a galloping horse in a pretend herd, an Indian chief, a jungle explorer.

I am a builder - child-like things, a library of my storybooks, a theatre, a hospital for dolls, a tree house. Later: I learned building takes a crew. So came the children and family, an organization, community projects, collaborations, and creations.

I am becoming a wild child again.

I am a performer. Madam Sophia, a fortune-teller for my grandchildren's Halloween parties.

I am a traveler, happy to plan, pack and go—seeing the colors of new landscapes, meeting friendly people, and discovering meaning through these experiences.

I am enjoying new and wonderful things in the beauty of each day—the unfolding of possibilities, surprises, creative and unpredictable rhythms.

I am lucky in so many ways. I have a solid husband of nearly 50 years and three daughters, two beautiful grandchildren, and dear friends, all of whom warm and sweeten my life.

I am grateful for my life full of grace and love, and for family and friends who have freed the wild possibilities within me, as I hope I have done just a little bit for them.

I am an unfinished work; I am emerging and embracing what is and what is yet to be.

Play Your Own Game

CAPABILITIES

I was born in a little college town in western Indiana in the mid 1950s. This was the pre-civil rights era, and there were things as a child that I was exposed to that I didn't fully understand, mostly around the restrictions that existed for women and minorities in my own small town. I grew up in a family much like the once popular television show, *All in the Family*. I loved my parents, and yet this is a classic circumstance of "hate the sin and love the sinner."

One summer I wanted to invite a boy I played baseball with over to our house. He couldn't come because he was different. I liked the kid and we wanted to be friends. To me, he was just another nine-year-old boy, except he was black. I am still a little emotional talking about it. I could associate with him on the baseball field, but there were clear limits about where we could associate beyond that.

I just didn't get it. Being exposed to another good person, a kid that I wanted to be friends with, only to be separated from him for what I could see was no good reason, bothered me then and haunts me even now.

You can choose to live life from the bleachers, but that's really not living. Get out in the field and play the game.

Years later I was working, running a $350 million business, when I was contacted by the CEO of one of our large clients. He was calling to invite me to an executive breakfast in support of an organization for which he was chairing a fundraising event. The organization had been founded by a rabbi, a priest, and a minister to help heal interfaith divisions in New York City. (It later expanded its scope to fighting bigotry, bias, and racism in America). Though its roots were faith-based, the organization chose to focus on those things we have in common, as opposed to the more outwardly obvious characteristics that make people different. Over time, I became actively involved in their work. After two years, I was asked to take a seat on the board. Over the course of 10 years, I led the development committee of that organization and became a part of the executive committee before retiring from the board as vice chair and becoming director emeritus.

One of our slogans was "nobody is born a bigot." We grow up in an environment with the prejudices and biases that exist around us, so there is obviously a nurturing component to how we think and feel about things. As young people, we don't have the skills to necessarily resist bad guidance. For better or worse, we are our parents' children. Also there is an unfortunate tendency for people to seek out the comfort and safety in being with people just like them—whatever that means.

There is a fear of the unknown. Yet through life experiences and maturity, we have the opportunity and the responsibility to determine what are constructive or destructive attitudes and belief systems. At the end of the day, people have to pick what's right for them; it is a fundamental and requisite point of personal maturity. Many of us have much of the same "inputs" (public school, media, friends, family, books, etc.) and yet people choose to react to them differently. People are often reluctant to take a stand or pick a side.

There is no doubt people can change. However, only they can ultimately make the choice to change, no one else can do that for them.

Almost everyone resists change. I have seen that often in my professional life, during which I have had the opportunity to lead many change management and business transformational activities. Change means that there will be discomfort involved. It can be extremely painful, but that's part of growth. It's the preservation of the comfort zone that holds people back from changing.

The scale has to tip related to the price people will pay for change. Whether it's abandoning an old idea or realizing more gain (material, emotional, etc.), people have to see why they are holding onto a current or previous position or attitude and the value they derive from holding on to it. They have to understand inside themselves that there is substantially more value (emotional, intellectual, material) in whatever change they must make than in staying planted where they are. Until they see and believe that for themselves, they are not going to move.

With more than 15 years of acquisition integrations under my belt, I discovered a pearl of insight. Resistance to change falls into two main categories: one category is habitual resistance and the other is malicious resistance. This is critically important, because my experience has taught me that habitual resistance can be dealt with by using the correct approaches, and then those behaviors can be changed. Malicious resistance, however, is far more difficult and damaging—you might even say impossible to change, at least in any reasonable time frame that you will have professionally to effect change. When you are the person in a leadership role, making this diagnosis as quickly and correctly as possible may be the single most important factor in determining your long-term success as a change leader. In the case of the habitual resistors, there is willingness to grow through discomfort for the greater good. The malicious resistors don't really care about the greater good, because it's more about them. They are not willing to go through the discomfort for anyone. They will try to influence others and become the virus to change.

I often refer to this as being the difference between being stunted or stuck. If you're stunted, sometimes that's a matter of choice. The idea that "I am who I am, so take it or leave it," can be very self-limiting. Then it becomes about reaching out and being willing to be open to other points of view and other people. For me, holding onto that idea, and trying to develop and nurture those skills in myself, has opened up relationships for me. There is great joy in getting to know someone else's heart.

In a sense it's about being a life-long learner. I think there is something that is planted in some of us that speaks to being a bit more of an explorer. But that can also be developed through self-awareness...if you choose. The more diversity, breadth of thinking, innovation, and ideas you can welcome into your life, the more you add texture and content to your world.

Being in a position of leadership means being in a position of servant leadership.

I don't think many people teach leadership anymore; they teach and model management. And in truth, you don't really manage people—you lead them. When you try to manage them, you ensure sub-optimized results. Because if it's more about you than it is about the other person, you will always be a self-limiting and sub-optimizing leader. It's not about you; it has to be about something more. Whenever leaders care about other people more than themselves, when they see and share a higher order of things beyond themselves, then people change and things transform much more quickly, driving better results.

It's a fact of life that many people who land in positions of leadership have big egos. It's also a fact that 70 percent of people in organizations are not effectively engaged in their jobs. Through the leadership principles that I have emphasized you can raise engagement in a phenomenal fashion. This is more common sense than people think; I scratch my head at times wondering why this gets lost. We live in the most highly educated society in the history of mankind. But we have been educating people's brains, not their hearts. We need to connect them, not separate them.

With a little exposure to people, if you are at all observant, you will be able to know what they really believe in. Usually it takes time and really focusing on what a colleague of mine likes to refer to as the "Say-Do Ratio."

The "Say-Do Ratio" demonstrates commitment and conviction with observable evidence and is the ~~cornerstone~~ of authentic passion.

Leading change is not an academic or intellectual exercise. You must lead from the heart. Business leaders are seeking better bottom line results, yet their approach unintentionally sub-optimizes what they can potentially achieve. They become so focused on results and hitting the numbers that they squeeze out the importance of employee engagement. Employee engagement is not an intellectual exercise. Look to examples outside of business where massive change has been effective by the likes of Gandhi, Mother Theresa, Martin Luther King, or Nelson Mandela. These movements, where the leaders faced powerful and deeply rooted change resistance, led change with little money and no formal resources, and they were all in environments where the odds were grossly stacked against them. But they found something in people's hearts. You can touch people's hearts in business, if you do not allow yourselves to get lost in all the metrics and measurements.

KNOW WHAT'S IN YOUR HEART, BELIEVE IN IT, AND GIVE THAT GIFT TO YOURSELF AND OTHERS

I Am

I am from small town America, not Mayberry RFD, but it might as well have been.

I am from Bob and Virginia, their first of two sons, descendants of early settlers who landed in Philadelphia only 80 years after the Pilgrims landed at Plymouth Rock.

I am from agrarian parents who either grew or killed every piece of food that hit their plates for the first 20 years of their lives.

I am from a father who was a Navy sailor when I was born, drove a home delivery bread and bakery truck until I was five, and over the next 20 years worked his way into a white collar job.

I am from a home where Mom was almost always there, offering support, encouragement, and a strong sense of assurance that we were only limited in life by our willingness to study hard, work hard, make good choices, and worthwhile sacrifices.

I am from a childhood where fun was Little League baseball, hand-churned ice cream, skipping rocks on the lake, collecting cat's-eye marbles, and watching black and white TV with three (maybe four) channels. Oddly enough we were never bored.

I am from the Beatles, the Rolling Stones, Jimmie Hendrix, and Woodstock. I am from love-ins, sit-ins, Kent State, and race riots.

I am from Big Blue, the Big Red Machine, big hair, long hair, Pong, PAC Man, pinball, Peanuts, Pogo, Popeye, and "plop plop fizz fizz—oh what relief it is."

I am from more than 20 Indianapolis 500 races, AJ Foyt, Parnelli Jones, Mario Andretti, the day Eddie Sachs died, and the introduction of the turbine engine. I am from Churchill Downs, the Kentucky Derby, thousands of hours of handicapping, and "run you stinking bag of bones run!"

I am from a personal transition of being strong and stoic to growing and knowing the pain of too much tenderness. I am from a place of adequate experience to know that I have "feet of clay." I have learned the redemptive power of forgiveness, and in that process, I have learned that people who do not agree with me are right more often than I care to admit.

I am from community service—actively fighting bigotry, bias, and racism—losing some friends, but gaining better ones along the way.

I am from being open to new adventures and opportunities that have taken me from the "out-house" to the White House and pretty much everywhere else in between.

I am from discovering that hugs are far better than handshakes, thanks to my Italian wife. I am from the realization that the best name I have ever been called is "Dad."

I am from a place of quiet optimism. I believe the journey is every bit as important as the destination, that fun is the by product of a job well done, and that happiness is a "choice."

I am from never forgetting my roots and never limiting the reach of my branches.

◉ **Rob Knauer** ◉

Imagine No Limits

INNOVATE

In 1956, during the Hungarian Revolution, my family escaped from Hungary. The Communists had taken over in 1944, changing all of our lives. Our freedoms and property were taken away. My grandmother committed suicide and my younger brother died; it was a bad time. The mind control of Stalin's regime was strong and relentless. Our newspapers were controlled, and we couldn't listen to Radio Free Europe. They even published new textbooks in schools and adapted them to what they wanted us to believe, and they changed the history books.

In 1956, the college students in Budapest organized an uprising against the communist regime. My parents did not see any way that this revolution would end well. I was 15 when they decided to escape to Austria and hopefully get visas to the West.

Escaping was a huge undertaking with many possible pitfalls, including getting shot at the border. To get there we had to walk most of the way, avoiding deep trenches and fences that were lined with explosives. One morning in October we set out on the trip to freedom—four sisters, my parents, and myself. I remember the land was so beautiful—covered with snow, haystacks sticking out. The soil had already been worked and was frozen in small peaks and valleys, making it difficult to walk. Each of us had a little sack we took with us. Inside my sack was "krumpli cukort," a sort of potato candy.

When we got to the border, we saw American soldiers in uniform standing on the other side of a six-foot trench. My father was worried there might still be mines in the bottom of the trench, so he threw us across it, one by one, to the soldier on the other side. The soldier gave us Hershey bars that tasted so wonderful. This soldier was the first black person I had ever seen.

The Austrian government had set up a large camp for all of us with sheets hung up for walls and piles of hay for mattresses. I remember I have never slept so comfortably as I did in that uncomfortable situation. I knew we had a goal in mind. As long as I have an end goal, I will do what it takes to get it done. Hard work doesn't scare me. My Mother often said, "If it's worth having, it's worth working hard for it."

We had escaped late, and the United States immigration quota was full, but we somehow got our visas and flew to New Jersey on January 1, 1957. I looked out the window as we flew over New York and everything was so shiny, colorful, and bright. It was exactly how I thought America would be—the streets looked as if they were really paved in gold. Later I realized that these were the Christmas lights.

Coming to America was like getting a brand new book—I wanted to learn everything about it without worrying if my parents were going to approve. We eventually settled in Allentown, Pennsylvania. There the real hard work started—learning the language and customs of America where life was different, and I wanted to be part of it. I learned to assert myself and forged my own way instead of following Hungarian customs. I learned English, did well in school, and settled in.

All these accomplishments gave me strength and created a foundation for the rest of my life. I married, but as I think back, I realize that my ex-husband never had any experiences like mine and eventually it drove us apart. Our approach to problem solving was very different. When our son got really sick with juvenile rheumatoid arthritis and the doctors said he would be dead soon, my ex-husband accepted what they said, but I didn't. I was shocked that he was not willing to examine other possibilities. I wanted to examine all possibilities, not stop just because a doctor said to stop. My ex-husband didn't think he could figure out his own answers, and he accepted what everyone told him.

When challenges seem huge and impossible, break them into smaller pieces and they will be easier to deal with.

I researched our son's condition, took him around the country to various doctors, and kept searching for the answer. Today my son is an accomplished adult with an advanced degree, married, and happy. Seeing my son's progress gave me confidence to trust my gut instincts.

At one time, my son was locked in what some said was a permanent fetal position. I was told that he couldn't be operated on. But I kept asking, "Why not?" and eventually I found a doctor in Washington who was willing to explain the challenge: my son was still growing and there were no prosthetic hips for his size.

Our solution was to make these prosthetic hips. The surgeon got on the phone with my father, who was a mechanical engineer, and my father made the prosthetics. My father and the surgeon would send the model back and forth until it was ready. The final step was to take the prosthetic hips to a jeweler to polish the ball of the hip. When the surgery was done, my son came out laying flat. So amazing.

Regarding my son's condition, I was very clear about my goals. One specific goal for my son was that he be able to walk with crutches in the house and use his scooter outside. If he had to use the wheelchair all the time, it would be a different reality for him, a more difficult existence. Being able to use crutches in the house would give him a lot more flexibility.

My sense of fairness and looking beyond the façade to find people's strengths got fine-tuned by fighting for my son. I also learned how important it is to smile or laugh, even during serious times. It gives the mind a break, which it needs during tough times.

My approach has always been to jump in and work out the problem. An example is when I organized a juvenile arthritis organization that included parents and professionals. My purpose was to get the kids, parents, and doctors together to talk about the disability and offer advice and support. This creates a community around the child with the goal of helping this person be whomever they hope to be. At first we had about six people present. This group has now grown to 850 parents and holds annual conferences.

During this process, I learned that to make change happen, it is important to work with the person who has the most power. Secondly, be nice to the people you deal with.

I learned to listen to people that I respect, and I learned how to bounce back from plans that don't work out well. I learned that there is not much that scares me.

Eventually, I was offered a job with a non-profit agency for disabled people's advocacy. This agency was on the brink of shutting down, and the board of directors gave me six months to see what I could do. I loved the challenge and did well. I reached the goal I planned for. The agency turned around and became the largest, most well respected service provider for the State of Washington.

Leading from behind is about finding out what people do well and putting things in place to support them.

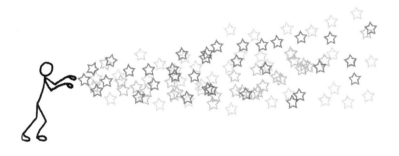

Passion is essential. I was passionate about helping people with disabilities reach their goals. I was happy to have the opportunity to create a well-run company with a good working environment for staff. I wanted to have fun and create an environment where my staff's personal goals would be honored and supported. If they are not happy, then I have to watch them all the time, and it's a waste of time. With all projects, I get staff involved in the process early on and bring them along throughout. Coming in and telling people what they should do just builds resentment. I wanted people to grow with me, be excited about the project, and be part of it in an organic way.

The nice part of being an executive director is that you can change what you want to a large degree. I like being in control, and I am willing to take the negatives that come with that. After 24 years of being the executive director, however, I was exhausted, wiped out emotionally and physically. I paid a friend to do a Person Centered Plan for me to shed some light on what I might do when I left this position. The outcome was that I should look into teaching. Then another friend asked me to come talk to her class at the university. I was energized by this experience. I worked hard to impress the students, and my talk worked out fine. I was offered an opportunity to teach one class. I was new to this, but it was a challenge, so I jumped at the opportunity. I worked for the college for 16 years until I recently retired.

During my various advocacy steps, I was often told "it can't be done." Of course, that would be exactly the challenge I would take on. I always enjoy a challenge. It is the pioneering spirit. I have always questioned the status quo. I was known in my circles as the "Why Not" Lady.

Change can be exciting. It is all about what you want to do, what role you want to play, and whether you want to be involved in change. If I lost everything, I would not be afraid. I would figure it all out. I wouldn't be passive about it. I would research, create a goal, and follow my instincts.

I Am

I am a person who wants to understand the world around me.

I am happy when I can get dirty hands from working in my garden.

I marvel at the beauty of planting a seed, and with time seeing it develop into a beautiful blue flower, Himalayan Blue Poppy.

I am in awe of the gifts the four seasons offer us.

I am proud that both my children have advanced degrees, are happy, and have found their places in the world.

I love it when my family loves me.

I am proud of my accomplishments, especially those when I was in a leadership role.

I am one who values teamwork.

I am curious about human behavior, why we behave the way we do, how we can impact change.

I am aware that there are many people who are doing without, who are hurting, who have no families. Makes me sad.

I wonder about the kind of a God who allows for such injustice, especially among children.

I am trying to determine my focus in my retired life.

I am looking forward to finding someone, a partner, with whom I can share my life.

I am working on making new friends in the community where I have recently relocated.

I am confident when I am given a project to complete that I have the skills required to put together a team of people who will get the job done.

I am much like a conductor of a great orchestra with the end result being a beautiful piece of music, a well-done job.

I am, most of all, mom to my two children. This is my greatest achievement.

I am looking forward to completing the transition from single breadwinner for 35 years, to enjoying my retirement.

BARB BARRETT

Other Side of Fear

RISKS

My first ego collision with reality happened when I was 31 years old and was diagnosed with breast cancer. The message I heard was, "Look, here's proof that you are not as strong as you present yourself to be." This experience, a confrontation with my own mortality, forced me to be more honest with myself about my vulnerability. My second big ego collision was with the painful break up of the 13-year relationship with my son's father. I had been in denial about the fact that this relationship had lost all of its nourishment for me. The relationship fell apart in ways that mirrored my own dishonesty about what I needed and what I failed to ask. These events broke the illusion and shattered my projection of reality. Life, and the people around me, were no longer what or who I thought they were.

Up until breast cancer, I believed I was a politically savvy operator, meant to lead in the conventional sense of the word. Breast cancer shattered all of the assumptions about who I was. I was mortal, human, and frightened. In the aftermath of a brush with death, the projection you're living with almost always falls away. You can either stitch it back together as it was, or you can sit longer in the void, where there are no projections, or a brand new projection comes in, which always happens over time. Your new projection—your new ideas and beliefs about who you are— will start to form a new reality for your life.

I remember saying to my partner at the time, "I can't go back to politics, it's totally not me, and there's something else I'm supposed to do." I think he expected that I'd just go back to work as the person I had been before, but I couldn't do that. I needed to make something more beautiful and be more connected to my innate nature.

Before breast cancer, I could not feel the disconnect as directly. It was more subtle, like a general malaise. I was performing at a high level, being acknowledged for my leadership performance, and I wasn't truly uncomfortable until I thought I was going to die. It was the first time I had a profound experience with the void. And without it, I could not have seen a version of myself that was closer to my core.

Truly new ideas, new concepts, anything new, comes out of the void.

If we run away from ever experiencing the void, we will stay the same, our realities will reflect that sameness, and real change will only happen when it's forced upon us. This understanding of the void has been critical to my style of facilitation. I try, in as many ways as I can, to help people experience the transformative, creative potential of a void.

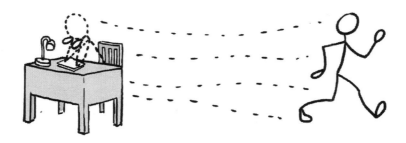

I remember sitting at my desk when I was working for the mayor after having just completed all my chemo and radiation treatments, and someone asked me, "What are you going to do now?" I said I didn't know, but that it would have something to do with kids and art. I couldn't explain it then; I just knew the idea was pushing through me and it would not go away. I left the mayor's office shortly afterward, and I started writing.

Through my writing my new sense of self and purpose emerged. This new thing I was going to do was different from anything I had done in the past. It felt a lot like jumping off a cliff.

Some people dismissed me or called me naive. Others were inspired. My mom was delighted because she could see it was more "me." I lost a community of people but I gained an entirely new one.

The thing about taking leaps of faith in your own personal journey is that there will be plenty of people who don't understand what you're doing. Living this way is not always easy because you will disappoint people, or at least challenge their ideas of who they thought you were.

With this shift, I started to own my soul's need to express itself in art. I believe that all of us, in our core, are artists yearning to make symbols that mean something to ourselves and to others, to live free of the fear of experimentation, to be willing to come to everything with a certain amount of innocence, so we can truly innovate. Living this way is living truer to your innate nature. Because it's a process, it's likely you will, from the outside, appear to be changing a lot. I feel like I'm changing all the time and challenging assumptions.

I'm not afraid to change my mind about a host of things I thought I believed. People find a lot of comfort in defining things. But if you change as I often as I do, it's hard to define me and pinpoint what I'm about.

There's a very strong relationship between personal growth, adaptability, living through change, and the concept of freedom.

I've often debated with myself, weighing which was more important: love or freedom. I tend to come down on the side of freedom. Freedom is such a deep desire in us. It manifests in so many different ways. You can see it in the creation of this country. An arts organization that I founded after leaving politics, had the tagline, "Freedom to imagine and courage to be." The phrase, "freedom to imagine," really resonates with me. So often, our brains trap us in worlds of perception that are limiting or constraining to our growth and expansion. We live in prisons that are just a creation of our minds presenting the world as "the way things are." To take the space to peel back those layers might be seen as a luxury, but it's really a gateway to freedom that everyone has a right to access. Our old unconscious patterns don't have to shape our reality. Other people's opinions, social contextual reality, all of that feels too constricting in the face of the desire our souls have to be free.

I just wrapped up a nine-month group process, leading a team of 12, working for the city. There was a high level of dysfunction among them—divisive, fractured, undirected, apathetic, blaming, etc. Some of them had been in the same position for 20 years, working from very rigid assumptions, and had little openness to change. Everyone appeared to be starving for a healthier work environment.

Initially I was asked to do one retreat on creativity, to facilitate a "reboot," and to help team members see each other in a new way. We did that first retreat, and they were able to experience what it was like to be in a more open, collaborative space. Because

91

the team's manager knew we had only scratched the surface during this kick-off retreat, they asked me back to facilitate a process to keep the changed dynamic going and to define their overall vision. We melded culture change with a process focused on setting benchmarks, and it became an integrated approach. Given the personalities and the group dynamics, I consistently relied on more improvisational approaches to the process. It was clear the human beings in the room did not want to be manipulated into new behaviors. They had to arrive at any sustained change from an intrinsically motivated place.

One of the takeaways from that retreat was that it's essential to have a very general structure, but to allow for a significant amount of unstructured time, trusting in your abilities as a facilitator to improvise. If you come in with too much of an agenda, it leaves no room for the magic to happen. I've gotten to the place where I know just how much of a container to create.

Groups I work with always set their own ground rules from the beginning. Every time we get together we revisit the basic ground rules for how we're going to treat each other, how we're going to show up. I facilitate the articulation of those agreements, remind people of what they've agreed to, and support members of the team to self-regulate. In every case, people want an atmosphere of care—in particular, one where everyone takes responsibility for the emotions, reactions, assumptions, and perceptions they carry into the room.

We can all sense the oppressiveness of a culture where the needs and perceptions of the few dominate the needs and perceptions of the rest. An atmosphere in which we are more accountable, and consistently gracious in the face of difference, is a more creative environment.

It's important to clarify that it's not about suppressing conflict. The ground rules that we establish are primarily there to help us when conflict arises, which it always will. In some ways, as a facilitator, you want to encourage authentic conflict, but not without offering the group tools to do conflict well.

CONFLICT IS A BEAUTIFUL CAULDRON FOR CREATIVITY

Change often happened within the context of a meeting or retreat when there were moments when a person experienced what it felt like when things were done differently. For instance, someone would be acknowledged with gratitude and respect for something he or she did or said. In these moments, the tenor in the room would change to one of kindness and a generosity of spirit—and everyone could see how their actions, however simple, could change the tone of a room to positive or negative. If a moment happened where the level of energy shifted in the room, I would stop everything and have people reflect on the change, to speak to it, and be in the experience.

People have to feel change cellularly, energetically—to breathe it in. They can't get it cognitively. They have to be in it, like a stew.

A facilitator of change must be neutral, must have integrity, and must be willing to challenge anyone—regardless of power or position—with gentleness and compassion. All psychological literature says that intrinsic motivation is important for people to change. People don't change unless they want to. So if you, as a facilitator, don't allow people to come into that space and be intrinsically motivated to change, then your ego can push people back. Of course, facilitators are also human beings with distorted perceptions and past baggage. We're going to get triggered; we are going to lose our neutrality. We just have to own it, be accountable for it.

I've never been compelled by, and I don't necessarily trust, leaders who don't reveal themselves. I think when I have inspired people the most, it's because I've revealed something about myself and made a connection. At the arts organization, I was leading to inspire and making change on a broad-scale, programmatic sense. I was very clear about why it was so important to me, and I articulated that "why" to any and all. I raised money, published articles, and motivated staff all based on the "why." I noticed that when I included my own story, when I brought my personal struggles to the front, my capacity to lead grew exponentially. It was so much more effective, because it was honest and self-revealing. As a facilitator, in the work I do now, I continue this practice. Whenever I ask members of the group to share something about themselves, I always participate and share from a personal place. Then others are able to see me in my humanity versus as a "cut-out" character. With this openness, we all have skin in the game, with equal amounts to lose.

Leaders can model how to learn and grow and adapt. It takes courage to be transparent about the fact that you had an assumption that was challenged and now you're not sure, and to be open to new ways of doing themselves.

I think more leaders need to show themselves as learners, and admit to not knowing everything.

I think we have to lose our self-consciousness about sharing the journey of change, helping others see the beauty in it that is parallel to the grief of loss. There is no change without some grief. It's not possible.

When I was leaving the arts organization, one of the people who started the organization with me asked, "Why are you leaving us?" I told her that I had to. I had something else in me that needed to emerge and I had to leave to discover what that was. I think the actions we take to fix, define, and make things more certain in a totally dynamic, ever-changing, ever-dying, ever-birthing cosmos are often the ones that hold us back the most.

My beliefs keep changing based on life experience. Just as a belief starts to settle in, it may get challenged. Our beliefs are just assumptions that we're making to understand reality. These beliefs shape reality and the way things transpire in our lives. If we hold to our beliefs too firmly, they can constrain change. A big part of our adaptability is honoring the fact that all of our beliefs are assumptions; they are not givens or facts.

When you challenge an assumption, you are challenging a belief. We depend on our belief system, more or less, in order to function. So when we have to grapple with the idea that not everything we believe is true, it is very destabilizing, very uncomfortable. Because we're often grasping onto things to fix them, or define them and to be a certain way, we don't tap into the natural flow, this river of energy that is always in motion, never fixed.

What lasts is not the change, as a static thing, but an environment that is conducive to sustaining on-going change. The idea is not just to allow change, but also to embody it. It's a way of existing.

I Am

I am significantly shaped by my experience as a single child of a single mom trying to keep a roof over our heads as a professional artist.

I am steeped in southern culture through both my parents, inclining me towards soul food, beignets, muffaletta sandwiches and loving hospitality.

I am a Pacific Northwest transplant who craves both the desert and the moist trade winds that blow through the channel separating Maui and Molokai.

I am a mother becoming more of an advisor to a burgeoning teenage son who inspires me with his profound wisdom and sense of justice.

I am devoted to humor and laughter as a religion.

I am passionate about people and the ways they express love and life.

I am deeply curious about how we access our highest potential as individuals and as a collective.

I am challenged every day to show up with an inner equanimity, trust, and expansiveness.

I am forever grateful to the hundreds of people I've befriended in my 47 years who have taught me (almost) everything about myself.

Lisa Fitzhugh

{4}

EMPOWER

Designs. Activities. Process. Approach.

Hold people accountable for results and position them for success by giving your full support, assigning ownership, establishing a clear direction, and creating avenues for them to see that anything is possible.

Pave the Way Forward

DESIGNS

Sometimes our greatest challenges present the biggest opportunities to learn about ourselves. In my case, it was the loss of a friendship I cherished for over 20 years that created a big shift in my life. This friend was a confidant, an ally, and my "go to" person. We spoke daily—she was fully integrated into my life and we had an incredibly strong bond. During the course of our friendship, she positively impacted me in many ways, including introducing me to Tae Kwon Do, which remains a passion to this day. But despite our long-standing friendship, there was evidence of dishonesty in her relationships with others. I chose to see what served me until I was personally impacted by the lies, and that had a devastating consequence to our friendship. The situation brought front and center my own naiveté and denial about things I didn't want to see in others. It shattered my reality and called into question everything I had ever known and believed about relationships.

Following these events, my "word of the year" became "Truth." I wanted to discover the truth about myself. How I want truth in my life and what I love best about my work. I started paying attention to what made sense for me.

At that time I worked in human resources. I realized I wanted to do coaching, so I started talking with people about it and setting my intention. I trusted my gut, had some conversations, and then took action to move forward. In 2010, I participated in a personal development program and went on to become a certified coach. That's when I began to feel the biggest impact of the shift that had begun two years earlier in who I am, how I show up, and how I look at the world.

I had ideas about what coaching was. I thought I was going to use my skills as a human resources professional to work with others in the same way, but with expanded theory behind me. During my training I was surprised that I could spend four days solely focused on myself. I had to keep coming back to that work the entire time I was going through the certification process. That work forced me to go deep, to explore, and spend time on me in a way I had never done before.

It shifted who I was and how I showed up for two reasons. Spending time on myself to learn how to be reflective created an opportunity for my personal growth and enabled me to release judgment. This was critical for my development and helped me change my perspective. Second, it created a new mindset about how I wanted to go through life. It taught me to be intentional about what I wanted in my career and life. It shifted my focus and perspective on how I viewed certain friendships, people that I dealt with, and the energy that I attracted and energy that I wanted to stay away from. Overall, I was a happier, stronger person.

I wasn't necessarily looking for change, and I would have been happy with a quick fix. My goal was to get to the other side, get through the program. Then I got slapped in the face about all the things I needed to learn, and that became an opportunity to explore how I wanted to change, being in control of what was shifting in my life. So I wanted to continue on that journey beyond a class or merely something I needed to be doing.

The experience with my friend was a pretty big catalyst. An event of huge magnitude like cancer or a big tragedy is not always required to drive change.

Transformation requires a certain level of discomfort to make different choices.

One of my greatest strengths is compassion and the desire to think the best of others. As it turns out, that quality is also one of my biggest weaknesses—one that I will always have to pay attention to. I have to question things a little bit more than I might have before.

I have also developed a stronger mind-body connection so I am aware when things are impacting me. For example, I had an eye twitch for a long time due to the stress, but it did not prompt me to confront the situation. I would not let that happen again.

There were times when I believed people could modify behaviors, but not truly change. This experience taught me that change is possible if you have the desire, the right tools to effect change, and the discipline to choose how you feel, how you act, and how you react each day.

Going through the coaching certification process helped me see how I confront situations, and brought my values more front and center. I became more accountable for how I show up—and all of those things I learned influence my relationships now. I navigate relationships with more ease. I see them as choice points.

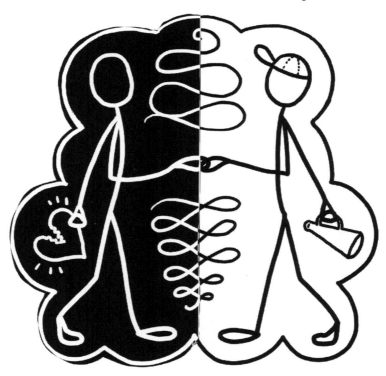

Now I look at things through a lens of possibility. It's still work to see that there are more possibilities than one can imagine, and to realize that for these possibilities to manifest I have to remain open. At any given point in life I have a choice. How will I react? What will I do next? Will I do what I want to do or what others expect of me? I know I have the ability to impact everything that happens in my life.

Recently I helped lead others through significant change at work when a well-respected leader left the company after five years. He had created a very strong culture, but not in a conscious way. This leader was focused on results and getting things done. He trusted people and led by being. He wasn't proactive about sharing a vision, but he was passionate about his work with the foundation and was 100 percent focused on the experience of the people we served.

Lead by example, make decisions, work hard, set clear expectations, and challenge others.

His departure had a tremendous impact on the organization and on me. I found myself stepping up in his absence to help lead others through the gap that was created when he left. He cared so much and had a lot of passion for his work. That made me consider my own work and why I do what I do. His influence was a reminder that it's important to focus on the work I am doing, the environment I'm in, and how I choose to spend my energy and time.

There were other leadership changes at the top when he left. The cohesion that existed within the leadership team was gone, and people felt adrift. It felt sad for many, like the end of an era. The focus began to shift to who was leaving the company next and

105

who was staying. There was speculation about the future, and fear about the shift in leadership style. Overall, this change allowed me the opportunity to step up in some different ways. There were many people impacted and no one telling me what needed to be done. It was a new experience for me to step out and take more risk. I was okay navigating on my own because I had the support of others in the organization, and it was the right environment.

I approached the problem differently than I would have before my coaching training. I came at the problem from multiple angles. I tried several different tactics versus a single approach to fit everyone. In the past I may have done a seminar on change, picked a model for managing change, and put the organization through training. This time we added small group discussions, held individual meetings, and engaged the other leaders about what made sense for their teams. I had more empathy and actively tried to meet people where they were. Also by not sharing my fears and trepidation, I became a positive role model for creating stability and embracing possibilities. I influenced others through my own behavior by modeling how to navigate change.

Everyone goes through change differently, based on past experiences and their connections to individuals or situations.

I learned that the time it takes for others to go through the cycles of change varies. When the organization was trying to press for "big 'C' Change" (get on or off the bus), it was not effective, because everyone was at different stages within the transition. That showed me not to judge a specific tactic too harshly, because timing and readiness is a factor in whether a tactic is effective or not. It promoted a "don't give up" attitude.

For me, understanding it's not all about the "big 'C' Change" approach enables me to be more persistent in my conversation with leaders, in sharing examples and stories of why announcing change does nothing to demonstrate change has actually occurred.

Sometimes change doesn't stick because you simply don't try long enough to create a new pattern or habit; or because it's someone else's idea versus exploring your own idea of what might work. Bottom line, if you are changing for someone else, you can probably modify your behavior, but it won't create lasting change.

I consider myself a reformed human resources professional because I conformed to a certain mold for many years. You can conform to a mold for a long time, but it is hard to be who you really are when you are changing to please others.

If you choose, you can live through ambiguity. If you do not choose to get wrapped up in speculation, and you have the confidence and skills to do your job well, things will turn out the way they're supposed to. Sometimes as hard as it is, change can be good for an organization. Through every change, something good can emerge. It's about realizing the possibilities. Without the ability to see possiblilities, change is a lot harder to go through.

I Am

I am learning to be unapologetic, to step out and say what I feel, to be who I am.

I am not afraid of the unknown, and am someone who sees possibilities.

I am passionate about helping people grow, and am actively practicing being grateful.

I am shaped by the work ethic of my parents, by their strength of character, and the challenges they overcame. I am grateful for the wonderful life they created for our family.

I am full of love for my husband, family, friends, and everyone who strives to make this a better world.

I am blessed to have a partner in life who believes in me, and supports all I do and all I pursue.

I am a Third Degree Black Belt in Tae Kwon Do, and am grateful to have found this life-changing pursuit.

I am good at leaping, metaphorically speaking, but not so figuratively.

I am fit, strong, and work hard to stay that way because it's good for my body and my soul.

I am a true warrior and work with others to discover their true warrior ways.

KIRSTEN SMITH

Become the Work

ACTIVITIES

Someone once asked me, "If you could do anything you wanted to, what would you do?" This simple question changed the course of my life. Feeding a strong desire to see new places, talk to people and explore the meaning of life, learning and relationships, I hit the road to write a book, called "The Learning Journey."

Moving and meaning have been driving themes throughout my life.

I have moved to and lived in many different places from the time I was a young child. New places have always offered me points of comparison on my search for the meaning of life, or education, or relationships. After I got my doctorate, I spent two years living in South Korea in the Peace Corps. Then I lived in Athens, Greece, for a year. After that, I got a job in Little Rock, Arkansas, teaching at the university. I stayed in Arkansas about seven years, then moved to Baltimore, and then to Chicago, where I worked for a technology company that was doing exciting and innovative things. I had a wonderful CEO. She asked me a question that changed the course of my life: "If you could do anything you wanted to do, what would you do?" I answered, "I would travel, see places, talk with people, see friends, and just live on the road." She said, "Well, why don't you just do that then?"

The first question that came to mind was, "What would I say to people about what I am doing?" She immediately said, "Tell them you are writing a book; everybody understands that." At that point I actually began the process of writing a book. I put everything I had in storage and packed up my car, including four seasons' worth of clothes. Some friends sent me on-the-road books to help me prepare, and other friends in the music community made me a theme song.

I didn't want my life to be chaotic. I wanted my life to be meaningful. There were ways for me to navigate while being happy and excited and comfortable, trying out different worlds, experiencing this freedom without a lot of downsides. I didn't have a model in someone else that I could follow; I had to figure out each of the little pieces. I planned ahead, coming up with solutions for the little challenges on the road. For instance, I arranged to have a couple send me my mail as often as required. I put everything I could into my smart phone and laptop, and I condensed everything else into one box that would fit in the trunk of my car. I found I just didn't need a lot of space for things. I could condense and compact and still have most of the things I needed.

The most radical change is becoming comfortable with extreme freedom.

Occasionally I didn't even know which direction I was going until I got behind the wheel of my car, and then I would make the decision and head out. Other times I would have a plan, looking a little bit further ahead, and arranging to meet friends. As I traveled, sometimes I stayed in inns or bed and breakfasts, but there were also times when friends would invite me to stay for a month, be part of the family, help with the chores, etc. This expanded the appreciation I had for my friends because I was able to enter their worlds for a short period of time. Many people would think that hitting the road without commitments would take a toll on relationships, but it did the opposite.

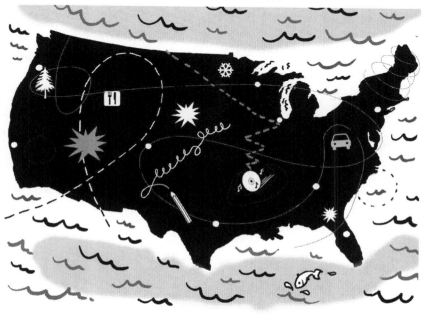

When I was about three-fourths of the way across the country, I got a call from a nonprofit in Atlanta that was helping low-income kids get into college. They had gotten some grant money. They were looking for an executive director, and asked if I would consider taking the position. This was exactly the kind of thing I wanted to do next. I wasn't quite ready to give up my time on the road, but I didn't want to miss this opportunity. So I turned my car around in the mountains of Colorado and went to Atlanta. I settled into nonprofit work for about seven years.

After several years of working for this nonprofit organization, I decided I wanted to return writing and living on the road. I spent about a year finding a way to merge the small nonprofit I was working for with a major organization, so that their work could continue and I could head out on my journey again. During that time I consolidated all my files into a laptop computer and a smart phone. Then once again I packed my car, this time with a little more experience. I had a car kitchen, car study, car workout room, and again four seasons' worth of clothes. I hit the road, and since that time I have been doing this Learning Journey for four years.

After about three years traveling without a safety net, I decided I needed a retreat. I now have a place up in the sky in a high-rise in Chicago so I can write in the sky and then hit the road again. I have interviewed over 100 people, visited many different places, and worked on the manuscript, finding that I enjoyed the writing. I am in no hurry to finish the book because it is such a great process.

I have always been attracted to the process of change. Moving and traveling are one type of change.

In my professional life, I've sought out situations where I could experience and lead change. When I was at university, I had a professor describe a time of change in his life as "The Golden Age." Arkansas was very much my "Golden Age." After completing my doctorate, I moved to Arkansas to serve as a consultant to the governor's committee to develop a learning experience for high school kids from around the state.

When I started, Arkansas had just elected a governor who was interested in education in the state. I was at the hub of a huge team effort that was able to effect broad change. I came in at just the right time with expertise on a topic that people were interested in gifted education. I wanted to make a difference in the lives of kids and teachers. I was able to design the master's degree program and to introduce a new gifted program. I set up summer programs that encouraged kids to learn new skills. The most exciting thing was that hundreds of kids told their parents and teachers that their lives had changed as a result.

One group of parents had worked for years trying to make change with little success. They had learned so much from the experience, and they shared that knowledge with me. I realized that putting an educational endeavor in place in Arkansas required not just an understanding of the actual changes being made in education, but also an understanding of the politics of the situation. I began to travel all over the state, building support. I was helping people communicate and understand the actions they would need to take to get the state legislature to give us millions of dollars.

Understanding a culture and creating a strategy for that culture is important.

Effecting change takes a team. You need to work very hard to figure out your strategy to make sure it fits the environment. We were able to draw on things that were part of the culture in Arkansas. There was a set of values that those progressive leaders at the time were admired for and they were seen as expressing independent views. There was a generosity that was part of the culture that was brought to bear. The community feeling was even more visible and appreciated as part of this program. You also need to think very hard about each individual and how he or she could be influenced. Each individual was an intentional part of the effort with us creating a unique strategy for each.

I encouraged graduate students to write three things they felt were important for gifted education in Arkansas. As a result of this process, they were energized by their own ideas, and the topic became a cause for them. Similarly, when I would do presentations out in the communities, I would start with a few minutes of listening to questions people had when they came in the door. Then during the speech, I would refer back to questions that they had asked. Connecting these conversations gave people ownership of the cause and helped create a community.

For a time, Arkansas was a model for how to get programs in education, how to find funding, how to roll it out state wide, and how to put in place a process that casts a wide net.

Sometimes opportunity for change comes because of a catastrophe and the need to rebuild afterwards. Sometimes it is because of a visionary leader. Other times there is just some sort of instability that occurs, or an organization or community is on the edge of something happening. Those situations, when a system is open a little bit more to change or the group has no choice but to change, are the times I would look for. I didn't mind swimming against the current within a structure or organization as long as there was a little support. I always knew I would have to do heavy lifting for a while. My rule of thumb is, "I am not called to succeed; I am called to serve."

EVERYTHING
IS
POSSIBLE
IN THE
IN-BETWEEN
SPACE -
WHERE YOU
LEAVE
SOMETHING
BEHIND
THAT HAS
BEEN
COMPLETED
BUT YOU DON'T
QUITE KNOW
WHAT IS
COMING
NEXT

Along with openness to change, there need to be some models to follow.

In the process of creating change, it was almost inevitable that I would run up against blocks of resistance. Things had been a certain way, and powerful people wanted them to stay that way. I tried to be clear and look for good models and metaphors to communicate. Even when I used my very best strategies, and had help from friends and colleagues, it was not uncommon that the block at some point would be insurmountable, meaning that those in power would say, "No, we aren't going any further with this." At that point I would go look for another opportunity.

I learned that by being enterprising I could land on my feet, explore something new, and turn that to my advantage, even in terms of a resume, rather than viewing it as just something that didn't work out at that time. Usually, I was able to have a good level of success before it got to that point. Once you get to a level of success with creating change, then it becomes more threatening for people who have a vested interest in a certain power structure. So, after a pretty high level of success, then there would be real resistance.

I know every day that I'm fortunate to be pursuing my Learning Journey. There is nothing that does not pertain to it. I feel as if I'm undergoing a special kind of training to remove my resistance to change. When each day is different, there is no way to become settled in one particular way of thinking. To be able to live in the sky and look at the clouds, acknowledging their lightness of being, is fantastic. I feel very fortunate to be on this path and stay excited about it.

I Am

I am a sojourner, spending much of my time on the road traveling from coast to coast and border to border, then retreating to write and reflect on what I've seen and what I've heard.

I am a dialoguer; there is perhaps nothing I enjoy more than a good conversation over a tasty meal with a friend or colleague or even a stranger.

I am a translator, spending most of my career converting theory or research into educational practices, or programs, or writings, searching for meaning through action and reflection.

Emily Stewart

Skip the Shortcuts

PROCESS

My life has been all about change. I have moved all over the country and taken on new roles on many occasions. But the most significant change in my life was bringing triplets into the world. Literally doubling the size of my family unit changed my life, my perspective, and my whole being.

I learned I was having triplets on my eighth wedding anniversary. I had an ultrasound, and even then I didn't believe it was possible I would have all three. Then on November 19, 2002, the triplets were born and life changed—my whole paradigm changed, both physically and philosophically. The physical aspect—the lack of sleep, the sheer organizational quandary of how you manage three babies with medical challenges, medications, etc.—is beyond what most people could comprehend. Your whole physical life changes, and you have to navigate the logistics of life in a completely different way. Nothing you are used to doing is possible.

The triplets came at 25 weeks. I was struggling, and had been taking lots of medication to delay their arrival. On the day of their birth, there were over 20 people in the delivery room with us. I knew our babies were very likely not going to survive because they were so small—each weighed two pounds or less. The doctors told my husband that there was a 60-70 percent chance the kids would not survive because they arrived so early. It was a miracle that they lived, and that they are beautiful, smart, and capable today. You get a new perspective on life when that happens.

I am a person who likes to be in control. With the triplets, everything was out of my control. I remember talking to the doctors about this after their birth. I asked if there was anything I could do to help. They told me that only time would tell, that each of those babies would fight as much as they could, and whatever happened to them would be their destiny. I couldn't control that. Learning there was nothing I could do to influence the outcome felt horrible. It's really hard to just be...and to wait, hope, wish, and pray. It felt exhausting. I had to recognize that I can't always make time move faster.

Sometimes we just have to be in the moment until it's over.

The models for change all suggest that you have to start with some level of dissatisfaction to create a burning platform for change. There needs to be something missing, a level of discomfort, or a problem you want to solve that leads to change. And even on a personal level, the greatest lessons in life are the hard ones. We don't learn as much from the things that come easy to us.

I have a propensity for change, so even if I don't have a burning platform, I need change because I get bored with the status quo. I like trying new things and doing something different. But the change I have driven in my career, in academia, and in my younger years is different than what happens when you have triplets at 25 weeks. That change is not self-induced; it is nature. It was out of my control.

The greatest lessons in life come from the things that are out of our control.

I thought with all the drama that came with my triplets, my career would be a distant second in my mind. But it wasn't. I wanted both an incredible career and an incredible family. When the babies were two, I accepted a much more demanding professional role, which was a crazy thing to do at the time, yet I was eager to try something new.

My passion for career, and my drive to keep learning and growing and doing new things, didn't change after the triplets were born. Despite how much I adored my kids, and how lucky I felt to have them, I still had this burning drive to further my career. I like to keep learning and growing, and that has never stopped. My decision to take this new job was difficult on my marriage; still I could not wait to aggressively pursue my career again when the kids were old enough to sustain it. That said, that experience brought me a lot of great friends, opened doors for me, and offered some of my greatest professional learning.

I have always been, and still am, a workaholic. But I certainly have a different perspective and appreciation for what it means to have children, and to realize how lucky we are, and what really matters in life. The older I get, the more I can appreciate that family matters most. My priorities around family are huge. I still spend a lot of time at the office, and I am extremely dedicated to my career and eager to grow and achieve. But my priorities are always present for me, and what matters most is my family. No matter what country or time zone I am in, I am always present for them. If they need me for something, I make myself available.

I have been working a lot on change professionally through teaching change management, and developing an executive leadership development program in partnership with some leading talent in the areas of executive development. We set out to create a program to build executive-level leadership capability within the company, and a key element of our program is how to understand, facilitate, and lead change within the organization.

In the beginning, we did a lot of listening to people, and we collected a lot of data to understand the existing set of circumstances. It's key to understand the change you are trying to create. Is there a burning platform for change, and if so, what is it? Who are the people who are interested in that sort of change? What insights can you gain?

Finally, we had to define where we were hoping to go with the initiative. We started slowly, creating small wins. With each of those wins, we got more and more people to come on board behind the idea. We also had to be willing to be wrong about some of our core ideas, and demonstrate a willingness to change course. We had to correct and shift according to what we were learning along the way.

In the organization I work for now, there are 14,000 people around the world in 62 different countries. Our desire is to become more collaborative globally, which means engaging more across city, region, and country to have a more collective feel for an organization that was previously more autonomous. We need enterprise-wide change to remain globally competitive within our industry. Our organizational change model is to create a guiding coalition of people who are behind the idea, and build momentum slowly by starting small. You celebrate small wins, share the stories, and go through all the steps.

There are lots of paths and lots of models, but no one right approach. In my organization, we teach people how to use five to six different models and encourage them to take whichever one works for them. There are a number of different paths, but you have to go through the entire process. You can't wing it and hope change will stick.

Current models for change work, but most people don't follow the steps. They get impatient and skip steps, then wonder why they don't realize sustainable change.

When I started to build the leadership program, we needed to start small and I had no budget. Now I am spending close to $500,000 on this one program alone. That happened because people started believing in it, and wanting to put money behind it. I never went and said, "Give me $500K." I started with no money, and when results happened, the company put some more money behind it, and it grew from there. It just shows that when you build positive momentum, more people get on board.

People can fundamentally change if they want to change. If they are not emotionally invested in making a change, they won't. They might get better for a month or few weeks, but it won't last. It's the emotional piece that must be present for change to occur and to stick.

Large scale, enterprise-wide change takes a long time. I don't think you make massive organizational shifts in a year; I think you make them in three to five years or more. We have been working on core leadership for three years and change management for one to two years, and we are just now starting to get momentum. The big challenge is disseminating the information when you have so many people, and are as distributed as we are. We have an approach—Learn, Do, and Teach. People learn new concepts first, then practice and reinforce them, and then ultimately teach others to reinforce their learning.

Rather than announcing big change, sometimes it's better to let things grow organically. In our organization, we try hard not to effect change through brute force. Our focus is to lead through influence, and get people to come naturally to a place of wanting to collaborate. Another key motto we follow is "good ideas just fly."

As I get older, I realize how important it is to balance my drive to do more with time to reflect on what's good in life, and to acknowledge the learning that comes from that process. The same is true professionally. It's important to stop and acknowledge how much success we have had, instead of only focusing on what we didn't do well, or why we are not moving the program further faster. It's also critical to ensure that we are not skipping any steps, and that we are getting to the emotional connection for people, not just the rational one. We want people to truly adopt the change, not just accept it.

I Am

I am from Sioux City, Iowa, and I am a Midwestern girl at heart with Midwestern values.

I am a daughter, a sister, a wife, and a mother, and proud to be all of these things in one person.

I am lucky enough to be among those with a college education and a master's degree, and I deeply value education.

I am Jewish, proud, and connected to this culture and history.

I am from a hard working father, without an education, who made his way to success through hard work and relationship building.

I am my father's daughter.

I am a networker and a connector of people.

I am a runner, a hiker, a skier, a piano player, a creative thinker, a philanthropist, a giver, and a friend.

I am a hard worker with an incredible work ethic and a lot of energy. This is my "secret sauce."

I am about embracing the global nature of the world, appreciating the broader context beyond just the boundaries of the U.S.

I am passionate about learning to speak different languages.

I am about being the best that I can be, and always continuing to grow and learn.

I am passionate about being a loving mother, mentor, and guide to my children, and loving them unconditionally.

I am lucky to be married to someone who loves me more every day, unconditionally, and who wants to be my partner forever.

I am still learning to love myself unconditionally.

I am convinced that family is the single strongest force in my life.

I am incredibly lucky to have the beautiful family and all the friends and the life that I do.

I am inspired about making a difference in the world during my time here.

Mindy Geisser

Help Others Shine

APPROACH

When I began thinking about the topic of leadership, I remembered one particular person who absolutely changed my life. I was about 25 years old when I met my first official mentor and business partner. I was working as instructor in a dive-instructing business in St. Thomas, U.S. Virgin Islands. My journey to the island involved a lot of synchronicity and walking through open doors.

It started in Colorado. I had graduated from college and was working in a psychiatric hospital with plans to attend graduate school. Both my parents were social workers, and I expected I would follow a similar path. I loved diving, however. Both my younger sister and I had gotten our scuba diver certification. On my refrigerator, I had drawn a picture of a beach and some structures and the ocean: my dream place.

One day my younger sister called and asked if I wanted to join her on an expedition to Caesarea, Israel, to excavate Herod's palace, which is underwater. I was just out of college, flat broke, so initially I said, "no," and hung up the phone regretfully. Then I reflected that I didn't get that kind of invitation every day, and I really just had to go! My Dad cosigned a $3,000 loan so I could go, and I did. It was amazing on many levels. I was so impacted by the experience that when I got home, I quit the hospital to become the first female dive instructor certified in the state of Colorado, and soon thereafter left to work in St. Thomas.

St. Thomas has changed now (so has the whole planet), but back then it was a magical place—very beautiful and free. After a somewhat eye-opening and rough start, I found myself working at my dream location—literally. The day I walked onto the beach at Secret Harbor I knew I was home, because I recognized it from the drawing I had put on the refrigerator. Explain that!

I worked for a couple who owned the dive center at a resort. In the 1980s, St. Thomas attracted a high-end tourist class. Scuba diving was in its heyday, and many of my clients were world-class executives. I had one diving client who was a wealthy Arab sheik. He brought all of his wives, daughters, and female servants for a custom trip to a deserted island where my dive boat met his yacht for their lesson. They had to enter the water with all their flowing robes on! I had another diving client who was an opera singer. When she was on the dive boat, she would stand at the bow and belt out operatic songs! That was the one instance where I truly loved opera—when she was singing.

Life was absolutely fascinating for me. One day I had a conversation with the dive shop owner. I told her that I wanted to do more. She said that if I reflected on it and gave myself a title and a job description, she would order business cards for me. I did just that. I gave myself the title of "Training Director" and that is what I became.

At 25, I decided I wanted to buy the business. That's when my first business partner changed my life forever. When the word got out that the dive business was for sale, that I wanted to purchase it and was looking for a financial partner, I was approached by a number of people. Of them all, my first business partner was unique, because he offered to become my financial partner, and to take the minority stock position. He also financed my majority stock position with a personal loan. All of the other candidates had offered me less than half. Maintaining control was important to all the other people who made offers. So, of course, I took my first business partner's offer! I became the majority owner of a business in a booming field that I loved, and it gave me a lifestyle that made me happy to wake up every day—all due to the generosity of this man.

Many "average" people are so involved with themselves, and keeping their own little light lit, that they don't often take the time to ignite someone else's inner light. That's why they remain average. Yet, there are people in the world who look for lights to ignite in others. It's my intention to always be the kind of person who helps others to shine.

When we help others shine, we are increasing our own Shine.

I think of this process as being similar to that of a small child who is full of the desire to explore life. All baby beings want to learn, to experience, to celebrate, and to explore. Simple observation tells us that this desire to expand into the astounding, world is hardwired into every living being on Earth. Hopefully, one or more adults will recognize a child's desire, and will help that child to explore whatever is going on in the moment— learning to walk, opening a door, mastering a game—all the many things we learn to do.

At a young age, though, we humans begin to grow beyond this open, trusting stage. We develop defenses and coping strategies based on the world we find ourselves in, which is, at first, based on our parent's behavior towards us. As we get older, we develop defenses based on our impression of how to survive, and thrive, in the face of all the different authority figures, social structures, and challenges we will encounter. I have observed that people begin to shut down, stop experimenting, and stop taking risks in order to survive and feel safe. Security has never been at the top of my values list. Sometimes when I think of my past, and wonder if I should have been a little bit more security minded, I have an opposite insight—perhaps I could have been even a bit more daring!

Thus far, I have had three careers. In some fundamental way each career has reflected my love of adventure and learning, a connection through shared values, and acknowledgment of the power of nature and imagination. In each venture I have started at the beginning, or bottom, and built myself, and the business, from the ground up. At times I feel like I am cyclically repeating Joseph Campbell's description of the hero's journey!

This process can be risky and at times hard on relationships and finances, but it is often where I feel most alive. My first business, the dive center, involved boats, navigation, safety issues, equipment, and weather, lots of water, creatures, nature, and people. My second business was a natural/recycled fabric clothing company that involved creativity, precise execution of the product, planning, sales and marketing, employees, accounting, economics, and national and global trends. In my third career, during the last decade, I have worked in the field of health and wellness, specifically as a yoga teacher and trainer, and as a weight loss coach, and educator.

Yoga teacher training has been a very exciting place for me to transform, and so, to transform others. I was absolutely happy while I was involved with it. Teacher training is a professional certification, yet it goes far beyond that. Part of teacher training is the process of passing on a body of information—spiritual, physical, emotional, intellectual—that is several thousand years old. It is ancient and wise, and has much joy and knowledge embedded in it. How all that information is delivered is really important too, and that's where I really came alive. My skills and natural talents lent themselves to the task of sharing this body of information in such a way that I felt joyful to do it.

I have traditionally shared this statement at the beginning of the second month of the teacher training process: "You're going to learn something important about yourself that you didn't expect to learn!" That happens to the vast majority of participants. During the two months together, a community is born that always becomes greater than the sum of its parts. Synchronicity starts flowing; healing and celebration start happening while specific skills are being learned.

Through my yoga career, I became acutely aware that one must continue to learn new perspectives and skills to stay fresh and alive. In order to learn new perspectives, the leader must make time to become a student again.

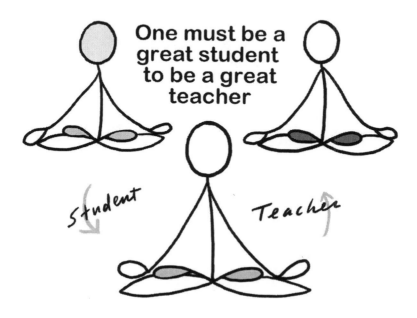

One must be a
great student
to be a great
teacher

Student

Teacher

There is a powerful link between excellence in leadership and emotional intelligence. For example, if a boss or manager (the person higher in the hierarchy) is angry, down, depressed, or in a non-resourceful state, his or her staff will react to those emotions in part by taking the emotions on themselves. They will become less happy and less resourceful. There is a direct link between wellbeing and productivity, so they will become less productive.

I am consistently amazed and dismayed when leaders miss this important factor. A keen observer can clearly see the effect that a leader with low emotional intelligence has on his or her organization. The world is full of things that can cause the most joyful person to feel anger, grief, despair, distress or more.

Excellent leaders have the ability to manage their own emotional states.

A leader must be able to choose a state of resourcefulness, regardless of outside factors. Resourcefulness has within it creativity, flexibility, compassion, and humor, among many other inspiring qualities. When a leader chooses to live in these states of being, he or she makes better decisions, and is the best leader he or she can be. Employees will be more inspired to perform at their best. Productivity is a natural effect of positive leadership. Life is such a precious short thing, and it is over for all of us so quickly. Why waste a moment being miserable, or making others miserable, if you can do otherwise? By focusing on their own happiness and balance, leaders help to make others happy. Everybody wins.

The leader and teacher in me are surrendering more deeply into my reemerging role as a student and an explorer.

The only person I can really change is myself, of course. As I change, my capacity to lead changes. I become more effective in delivering the gifts of spirit that are mine to give. I believe my spirit has a blueprint that remains constant. The major action that can occur over a life well lived is that the spirit can shine brighter and brighter, and thus illuminate all sorts of dark corners that could use some light and healing. The delivery system the spirit uses to do this may well change over time. As I open the door to new possibilities later in life, I am ever more curious about what my new delivery system will be.

I Am

I am from another place and another time, as well as from right here.

I am from a place where all things are connected, and where technology takes second place to human values.

My destiny seems to be, in my small, unique way, to help people remember that connection.

I am from a family of teachers, social workers, and ministers, with a bare sprinkling of entrepreneurs.

I am from two parents who left their religions behind.

I am half Protestant, half Jewish, but in truth, I am all earth-child.

I am more animal than I even know. In my inner animal heart, I wish to run free, far away from modern cities and towns, yet I am also a child of these modern times and a lover of people.

{5}

ADOPT

Success Factors. Develop. Brand. Communicate.

Ensure what you do meets the needs of the present without compromising the future by engaging, developing, and communicating to all.

Create Your Luck

SUCCESS FACTORS

I have represented low-income people for 40 years, including people with intellectual disabilities, institutionalized individuals, prisoners, juvenile offenders, welfare recipients, etc. I have represented a lot of people who are marginalized in one way or another. I have had a couple of sabbaticals where my wife and I did human rights work in the Middle East and the former Soviet Union. We served Palestinians living in the West Bank under military occupation and Roma living in Eastern Europe who were the target of discrimination.

Twenty years ago I was involved in the launch of a state Medicaid program that was designed to do many of the things the current Affordable Care Act (ACA) is intended to do. It was designed to significantly expand Medicaid coverage to the uninsured, to improve the quality of care for those on Medicaid, and to control costs in the state. For a few years, the program succeeded in reducing the percentage of uninsured residents of the state to one of the lowest, if not the lowest, in the country. It was also successful in containing costs. I played a supporting role, and from that position was able to watch real leadership being exercised for the benefit of people who usually are ignored.

Ten years later, I was involved in a failed effort to defend the same program from being dismantled. This was the most significant experience in my career. The dismantling of the state Medicaid program resulted in the loss of coverage for about 300,000 clients, and some of them died as a result. It happened because the people it helped were largely disfranchised and, in a political sense, didn't count for much. I see that playing out again in the current ACA disputes. There are states that are refusing to provide federally funded Medicaid coverage to people who are low income, people who are greatly devalued in our society.

I have had some successes and a good deal of experience losing. None of the other losses were as devastating as the cuts in the state Medicaid program enrollment; the stakes there were just enormous. There were so many people who had gained coverage and were going to lose that coverage. We knew the consequences of failure would be terrible, and they were.

The experience also changed me. I have been extremely privileged all my life: I have a wonderful marriage, an amazing son, lots of warm friendships, and a loving extended family. I had a great education and a happy childhood, and I've always been financially secure. These experiences colored my view of life. Even though I had spent my entire career working with people at the other end of spectrum, people who were being treated unfairly in many ways, I still had an optimistic view of the world. I had confidence based on my own experiences and professional success earlier in my life, when I watched things change for the better. The experience of the last 10 years has left me much less optimistic about things moving toward justice. I am still working full time on the same issues trying to get coverage for the same people who lost it 10 years ago.

I do feel a little disillusioned. I say that with some sense of embarrassment. I have a good friend who is now in his 80s with a deep faith commitment who protested our country's training of Latin American military and police forces that have gone on to commit human rights abuses. He consciously made a decision to violate the law in a nonviolent protest and be sent to federal prison as a statement of conscience. He was disillusioned by his prison experience. A friend of his commented, "Whoever told you that you have the right to be 'illusioned' in the first place?" To be disillusioned by that reality says something about setting unrealistic expectations.

Injustice often wins, and the weak and marginalized most often lose.

My clients' misfortunes are constant reminders that it is not about me. The tragedies that occurred in the state regarding healthcare affected a lot of people. Whether I was disillusioned or saddened by that, or my professional career suffered, is very insignificant in contrast to the suffering these people experienced. I have less faith in the judicial system than I did before. My religious faith is certainly less than it once was. But it would require dramatic megalomania to put those changes in the same conversation with what happened to my clients.

I grew up in an affluent family, taking nice vacations, and never had to be concerned about financial security. I went to an

145

elite college where I was the beneficiary of preferences for alumni's children, because my father and uncle went there. I got the benefit of all sorts of favoritism toward white males, because when I attended, there was an absolute bar against admitting women, and almost no minorities attended. But the greatest privilege of all was in being raised in a loving family: parents, siblings, grandparents, uncles and aunts, etc. I have a wonderful wife and child. I see clients who have never seen loving people in their lives.

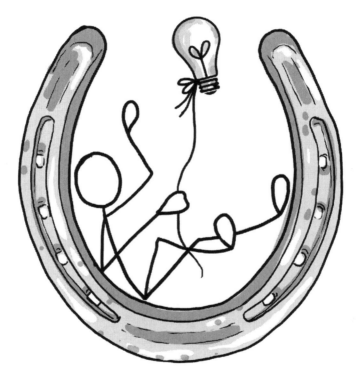

I believe it is always better to be lucky than smart. The things that happen to my clients—they are so unlucky, and I am so lucky. They inspire me with how they deal with their bad luck. I am still working hard on the same stuff on behalf of the same people, whom I tremendously respect. There are six million people in the state, which is small enough that individual relationships count. Staying in for the long haul allows you to develop relationships through which you can wield influence.

I love my coworkers and many of my clients. I represent people who have been dealt such bad hands by life, and are so generous and courageous. I love being reminded that there are good, caring, courageous people in the world. They don't quit, don't give up; they keep on keeping on. That continues to feed my soul and I am very grateful for that. The sorry state of the world can get you down, and you can become cynical. I feel like I am constantly drinking from the spring of goodness and decency that makes me glad to be alive.

Twenty years ago, I had close personal relationships with people in power, and I helped them exercise it on behalf of my clients. When that power was in the hands of other people 10 years ago, my ability to change the policies was severely limited. Relationships are critical to effecting change.

I suppose the experience gave me a large dose of humility. If you are trying to wield influence on behalf of poor people, you have to be opportunistic. You find opportunities to make your presence felt in the larger world, but you don't create that larger world.

An important relationship in my life was an older Civil Rights lawyer who is an extraordinary person. Years ago, we spent time together during a lawsuit that addressed inhumane conditions and brutality in the state prison system at that time. At the beginning of the trial, he taught me an important lesson, which was to never demonize your adversary. We didn't have to persuade the judge that those who lead the prisons were bad guys;

147

we only had to persuade the judge that the system didn't work. It made it much easier for the judge to side with us.

That was an enormous lesson that made it possible for me to credit the other side, and listen to the other side. The success story in the prison case was that the court created the space for people who worked in the system to make the changes that needed to be made. I couldn't have made those changes and neither could the judge. It was a matter of enabling the people working in the system—our "adversaries"—to make the reforms.

A KEY INGREDIENT TO CHANGE
IS JUST SHOWING UP

Class action lawsuits have well-documented limitations, but once you start a lawsuit, it has a certain life, and continues according to rules to a certain conclusion. In the prison reform suit, the media's attention would wax and wane over the 18 years, but the court was constantly engaged. State officials had to finally come to terms with reforming the prison system because the courts would not go away.

I am somewhat effective on Medicaid now, because I have 40 years experience on the budget process, and can mobilize the fiscal arguments to try to protect the program's beneficiaries. It is critical to just stay with an issue.

You don't accomplish anything by yourself. If you want to effect change in others, and you want it to last, you need people with shared values around you.

It is often observed by people that have experienced combat that it is allegiance to the people immediately around them, more than to some ideal, that keeps them going. There have been times when things have been very bleak and I have felt ineffectual, when the one thing that has kept me going is a feeling that I would be letting down friends if I gave up. Their sacrifices and support have made me get up in the morning and put one foot in front of the other. You need colleagues who you can rely on to call you out when you are falling short, inspire you by your own activities, and, on some days, reassure you that you are not crazy. "Power will never make concessions gladly," as Frederick Douglass observed.

If you are pushing against the powerful on behalf of the weak, you are going to get a lot of cues that you are not respected or likeable. If you don't have a group of friends that shares that struggle, you will not be able to sustain effort for change over the long haul. On the flipside, I have seen people working in organizations doing good work with good reputations, and the internal dynamics were not supportive. People would burn out in those environments. Find people who will support you and help you stay faithful to whatever you are trying to achieve.

with privilege comes responsibility

I Am

I am lucky. I was raised in a loving and affluent family. I got a good education.

I am involved with people who are usually ignored.

I am a steady worker trying to improve the lives of people who are marginalized.

I am less optimistic about things moving toward justice.

I am a little disillusioned, but I am no less responsible to right the wrongs that happen to my clients.

I am inspired by the people I represent—they feed my soul, and I am grateful.

I am showing up, and I will continue to show up, to effect change!

I am grateful to people around me: my wonderful wife and son, my supportive family, my colleagues, my friends—all of whom help me stay faithful to what I am trying to accomplish.

GORDON BONNYMAN

Make the Best Even Better

DEVELOP

A real mental turning point for me was when my husband flew off to Vietnam. He was a graduate of the state flagship university when young men had to be in ROTC for at least two years. He wanted to fly, so he became a pilot in the Air Force just as the Vietnam War was cranking up. On the day he had to go off to war, I dropped him off at the airport. I walked back to the car carrying our six-week-old baby and holding the hand of our two-year-old.

Along with my worry about my husband, it suddenly came to me: what would I do if he didn't come back? I had not finished college, where I was an English major with minors in French and art history. I had no qualifications whatsoever!

This was a different era. My parents, particularly my father, believed that boys had to go to a very good school (all my brothers, and my father and his brother, went to a major Ivy League school), but the girls would just end up getting married, so it didn't matter much where they went to school as long as they became polite, helpful women.

For high school, I attended a girls' Catholic boarding school run by cloistered nuns in Washington, D.C., where I met a number of lifelong friends. The school provided an excellent, if dated, education. Not many people have ever studied Greek etymology or memorized as much poetry as I have! After high school, I had been given a choice of living at home and attending the local state flagship university, or going away to a genteel ladies' finishing school college. I decided to stay at home. But that day at the airport, I realized that I didn't have the practical skills or qualifications to take care of my kids if anything happened to my husband.

All I could think of to do was to start buying the *Wall Street Journal* and reading articles about business. My father was a shrewd businessman with an understanding of stocks, bonds, and the law. He thought women should have some money of their own, and learn to manage their own money, so I guess I thought this was a first step. I have quite a few female friends who know little of their family's finances because their husbands handle everything. I agree with my father that this is not a good state of affairs for women.

My desire to understand business better led me to take a course in money and banking in the College of Business. I hoped to be able to understand the Federal Reserve System. Well, I made an A in the class, observed lots of cheating, and came to realize that probably the only reason the Federal Reserve System works at all is because no one understands it. I scurried right back to the English department.

Of course, I had to manage our money when my husband was in Vietnam, and that was a good experience. I like to joke that he went to Vietnam and never got the checkbook back! Truthfully, he still has a checkbook and makes plenty of financial decisions, but I do still pay all the utilities, etc., and I learned to make good investments.

When my husband came back from Vietnam, we had our third child, and he started his own business. I still remembered the feeling of insecurity when he was away, however. I continued my education, and earned a bachelor's and a master's degree. When I was a graduate student, I taught a few classes, and found I could relate to the students and was good at it. I wanted my students to love reading and learning from literature, history, and the arts. I always loved reading. As a child, I was told that I read too much. It was like dropping into another world.

I was energized by the things I was learning, and I found some really good mentors. They helped me to realize that I was bright. However, I knew that this work was only important to me, and that I needed to push myself if I wanted to get the degrees and teach others. I applied to a Ph.D. program at a university that was 110 miles away, and I was accepted. My husband thought that was fine, though my parents were afraid I would neglect my children. My routine was to drive the fourth grade carpool in our elderly Peugeot, then get on the road to drive to school two days a week.

I am very appreciative of all those who were encouraging to me. Of course, not everyone was encouraging. I remember asking one of my master's degree professors to write a letter of recommendation to the Ph.D. program. He warned me that I would probably break up my marriage if I went on with my education and that he wouldn't want his wife to have a Ph.D. Needless to say, I did without his recommendation.

After I got my degree, I was lucky to get a job at the local state university. I taught there for 30 years. When I first started teaching full-time on the tenure track, my salary was so low that my children would have qualified for reduced-price lunches in school, had I been their only support. Women were paid less than men at the university, and in colleges all over the country, but I loved my work, and I worked hard. In my years there, I tried to advocate for equity for myself and other women, and I do believe things are somewhat fairer now due to my efforts and those of other women.

I had to adjust in order to make the transition from working inside the home to working outside the home. I had to toughen up and grow beyond the polite, helpful Catholic schoolgirl and mother of small children into a professional woman.

I like to think that my experience of going back to school as an adult was helpful in counseling other adult students, especially women. I live in the Bible Belt, and many women's husbands, fathers, and pastors did not want them to go to the university. They warned them against liberal, godless professors, and the dangers of neglecting their husbands and children.

I really think some of the men in their circle were scared the women would become better educated than they were, especially when they had little education themselves. I encouraged these women to persevere and to be proud of themselves.

I learned a lot myself from seeing what difficult backgrounds many of the women came from. I only had to banish the specter of the Ivy League; they had a whole way of life to confront. I was also fortunate to pick out the right person to marry when I was only 20 years old. I have changed a lot over the 50 years of our marriage, but he has always encouraged me to follow my dreams.

"I have had a very fortunate life, mainly because I have been LOVED and BECAUSE I have had the Opportunity to Love others."

Much about teaching is really improvisational acting. I have a good sense of humor, and students seemed to like that. I tried to integrate all of the arts into my teaching of literature.

Books contain amazing insights about people. I sometimes wish I could prescribe George Eliot's *Middlemarch* or Jane Austen's novels to the powers that be in Washington, D.C., or our state capitol. Since I can't, maybe I can subvert their constituents with good ideas from great minds.

Literature reflects life, holding a mirror up to the reader to help her see the human condition better.

The great thing about teaching is that you are always learning yourself. Teaching is a license to learn. Every day is different. Every student is different. It is a privilege to be a teacher. There is so much out there to learn.

156

I Am

I am a war baby, the daughter of Isabel and Gordon, a young couple who married during World War II, were separated by that war for two years, but managed to raise five children and celebrate 62 years of marriage. I did not meet my father until I was two years old but was lovingly raised by my mother and four grandparents during the war.

I attended Roman Catholic schools for eight years; some of my religious instruction was good, some not so good. My religious views have evolved over time and are still changing.

My life has generally been one of evolution rather than a series of hard and fast choices.

My best choice was marrying my husband at a relatively young age; I was fortunate to be able to intuit who would suit me over a 50-year period.

I was fortunate to be able to go back to college as an adult and to have the privilege of teaching literature for 30 years.

I am lucky to have three children and six grandchildren who are the apples of my eye, and a large extended family whom I love. I have been blessed with good friends at every stage of my life.

I have been able to travel extensively and enjoy knowing people from other countries and cultures.

I am still learning.

Bonny Stanley

Feel-Right Passion

BRAND

I was fundamentally changed when I focused on someone else's needs, adopting them as my own. To explain: my oldest son is on the autism spectrum. With the help of trained people, both professionals and experienced parents, we realized we needed to act and think differently about our son.

Before my son's diagnosis, we were feeling around in the dark, trying to understand what would work. We had about three solid skills—head it off at the pass, avoid the pass, or pack it up. That wasn't enough. It impacted our social lives and his quality of learning.

During his early years—he's six now so I'm talking about the time leading up to two years old—we couldn't really see that we were parenting in reaction to his autism. But we knew that it didn't feel natural or mirror what other parents around us were doing. An example is that a dinner date that could be two hours for some families would be 30 minutes for us. Or an excursion out to a store with a play area would be a very tense 10 minutes, and then we were done and moved quickly away. We pulled back from really good family friends when we didn't know how to facilitate his behavior. Things like dinners, play dates, reaching out, just felt like a lot of extra work to make those things happen.

Over the course of many observations, we realized our son was different than most other kids. It would take about a year and a half to get an official diagnosis that he was autistic.

I feel like we went through two diagnosis periods. The first was the state assessment for his services. It wasn't an official diagnosis, but the assessment was comprehensive. That was emotionally difficult. We were finding our internal compass for terrain we'd never been in.

We were fortunate to find him the perfect school. The population at the school is half typically-developing and half not-typically-developing students. I spent that first year at that school with my hands being held—observing, participating, advocating, volunteering. By the time we met the second diagnosis period and received an official Autism Spectrum Disorder (ASD) diagnosis, he had been in school for over a year.

At the formal diagnosis, we were all in. We had come to a place of acceptance; we were ready to embrace the new. I made goal-driven meetings, asked the right questions, and created tools for my son's team. I was really ready to tackle the things we needed to get done and get in the driver's seat.

Here's my thought on making choices and embracing change— sometimes the choice or the need to change is obvious. Sometimes change is easy. Sometimes it's hard. For me, the need for change was obvious, so I put my ego to the side and rolled up my sleeves.

Parenting our son, and teaching him, required many skills and resources we didn't have. I needed to learn to navigate through information and resources. I expected there to be a ton of information and a certain level of bureaucracy. There are both. But there are also passionate people willing to help. They devote their lives to science, research, education, and advocacy. Their dedication and calling are staggering. And as our son has grown, we've grown, and our friends have developed their way of interacting with him, have gotten to know him, and it's become easier. Connecting with other people has been the most valuable thing. It's ironic because we were disconnected from people for a while.

What works today might not work tomorrow so keep it fresh and evolve your tools and skills.

161

Change is about being flexible, not rigid. I read the situation and see how our son responds to it. One of the things we learned is: if something's not working, we take it away or change it. We've been able to enhance our environment by putting routines around things or by paring down. For instance, I now assess how he's doing with his homework. He needs a routine and certain emotional space to make things happen. I noticed that when he was doing his homework in the evenings, after a long day, it was harder for him to regulate his emotions and to remain focused. So I started laying the process out in a certain order in the morning.

I saw results. But we still weren't getting to the last third of his homework, which is computer work. The computer was in another room, and between a crawling baby and other parental duties, supervising computer homework was more challenging than it needed to be. Then I set up a computer for my son at a small desk in the dining room. Success! It took fine-tuning over a five-week period, but now we've got a formula. It feels good and successful, and we're able to execute it every morning.

We have three social skill phrases that succinctly sum up my son's newly minted skills: "You get what you get, and you don't throw a fit," "Oh well, maybe next time," and "When you get fed up, get a grown up." The humorous adult translation of these concepts is something like "Get over yourself, it's not your time," and "Sometimes you need a team."

Regarding my son, we accepted that we need the support from a lot of people. When he was about three, we hired a full-time nanny. The search process was thorough, to say the least. I ran an ad. Of over 200 applicants, I directly responded to about 150. I did 14 phone screens, 11 in-person first interviews, and four final interviews. The three final candidates went through a four-round interview process that included working with our son for an hour, and the chance for candidates to have someone important to them meet and evaluate us. We found one perfect choice for our son and our family. He's been working with us for over three years.

Our son's team now includes family, close family friends, his school team, the nanny, the babysitter, his bus drivers, etc. If you interact with him, you're part of the team and we'll connect regularly. When things are a consistent struggle, we look around for a better way to do things. Sometimes we find a solution quickly. Other times it takes a little longer. But we always involve the team.

Find your right people and you hook onto great things

Parenting my son has definitely enhanced how I communicate with people and how I problem solve. At one point, I was participating in a topical three-month-long group parenting class, while in my professional life, I was leading 12 managers and 80 employees, managing a lot of workplace training and performance. My coaching and management style were naturally enhanced by my experience with my son. I learned a lot about expectations, clarity, and assessment. My approach to conversations was holistic. I naturally guided people through goal setting, step by step.

I've grown tremendously through this process. I deal with potential conflict so much better, and value the power of partnership and transparency even more. It's changed my thoughts on accountability, and really elevated my standard for action. It's changed the way I communicate. With a big team supporting my son, we need clarity. We need measurements for success. We need check-in points. We continually assess within the bigger picture. Context is key to clarity.

I've come to appreciate that everything can be bite-sized. When approaching drastic change, do it in small steps.

Think about physical therapy. You can be doing the same exercise over and over for four months, all the while feeling you're not making progress fast enough. Yet, it makes all the difference in the world. I feed myself by enjoying the smaller things in life. I set smaller, achievable goals so I can win often! We celebrate the small wins frequently. That's an important way we've shifted.

I've been able to make important things happen by being flexible, and being open to the call for change. Once I accept that the change must happen, I feel compelled to make the change happen. Despite all of that, there can be disbelief and discomfort. It doesn't feel good all the time. It doesn't always move along easily and quickly. You just make it happen with what you've got.

I Am

I am a student of learning, of understanding, of implementing.

I am a practitioner of change, of manifesting, of miracle making.

I am an admirer of self-reflection, of self-confidence, of self-love.

I am an advocate of self, of family, of tribe.

I am a consumer of failure, of iteration, of humble pie.

I am not striving for perfection or sole reliance.

I am not seeking praise, or popularity, or fame.

I am no more than I am, no less, no different.

I am honored to share my story with you.

Chris Guillot

Connect the Dots

COMMUNICATION

Only now, after years of relating to people, have I begun to share my own story and see the value in it. It makes me feel really good, as if I had tucked away something valuable in a shoebox for a long time. If it can help one person in 10,000, that is fantastic.

My parents were physically present when I was young, but their lifestyle was not what I wanted my life to be. They were there to make decisions, but I didn't trust the ones they made. I was about seven or eight years old when I realized my family life was a stark contrast from what others considered normal. Financially, we were less fortunate than others, and my father was in a motorcycle club where there was a lot of access to guns, drugs, and various criminal activities. My parents divorced when I was five, and my father was in and out of my life after that. My mother married nine more times to six different men, transitioning us from place to place with each new relationship. She would move to a different state, spend a few months getting settled, and then return to get us kids.

My grandparents on my mother's side were stable role models in my life. They were caring people who offered me a different way of living. They didn't have a lot of things, and they gave away what little they had to people who needed it more. It was never about them; it was always about others. When I was a kid I thought they made good decisions, so whenever I came to a fork in the road, I asked myself which way my grandparents would go. To this day, that has not failed me.

The summer of my junior year of high school, we moved from Arkansas to Kentucky, because there were better job opportunities there. My mother wanted to return to Arkansas at the beginning of the school year, but I didn't want to leave. I got a full-time job and found some people who would rent me the second floor of their house. I was 16 years old, living alone, while working full time and completing my senior year of high school. I excelled in basketball, and did well academically. I was the guy who could relate to all the different groups, so I was able to influence change in people who didn't even know each other.

I always felt I didn't have to be a statistic; I could reside in the minority of people who rise above their background. I didn't have to be an individual growing up in the kind of environment that would lead him to prison—as a criminal, or a drug or alcohol abuser. I remember thinking early on, "I have choices." I didn't know what I wanted to be when I grew up, but I knew what I didn't want to be. I put what I didn't want to be in a bucket, leaving everything else open. That influenced a lot of choices I made as a young adult. I didn't do the things other 16 to 18-year-old kids did. I couldn't afford to get in trouble, because there was no one there to bail me out. I made decisions to stay clear of all those dangers.

To me it wasn't something that was that difficult to do. It was right in front of me—I could be like my parents and indulge in that environment, or I could reject it and be open to other possibilities to change. What was difficult was living in that environment while making the change. Would I want to do it again? No. Would I change it? No. I wouldn't want to go through it again, because it was an emotional rollercoaster, but I wouldn't change it because I learned so much.

I am more open now than I ever was before. I am doing something I love to do: developing relationships all around the globe as an executive recruiter. The longer I work in this role, the more relationships become personal. Over time, mutual trust is created. It takes a lot of investment and openness on both sides to get there. I like listening to individuals, finding out what is important to them. It is not about the questions I ask, because there are no expectations.

> *Driving change starts with listening—just getting to know people, understanding them.*

I am on the phone a lot. One of the only things you can't communicate over the phone is emotion. You get to a place where there is a relationship based on trust and transparency. On a personal and a professional level my work is all about them. Seeing somebody's life change, and knowing I was a part of that change, gives me a sense of gratification, bringing me pleasure and fulfillment.

Individuals like to be heard. They want to tell someone how they reflect on a situation, what they think, how they see it. When you really listen to people and understand what they are passionate about, you may see that it may not be what they are currently doing. I was a master mechanic for 15 years, and I was really good at it, but it wasn't something I liked doing. Sometimes people may want a different structure or a different industry. I

169

collect that information and put it away. Later, I'll be working on an assignment that has those elements, and it becomes a matching game.

One of the things I have been working on for the last three years, which is the next evolution for me, is to live for my intentions, rather than my expectations. It changes my outlook on so many things. I find it so peaceful. For example, in the past if I went to a nice restaurant, I expected good food and good service. But those were all expectations, and I was setting myself up to be disappointed. It was already a negative. So I have changed the thought process. Now my intention is to find something that is enjoyable about the evening—if not the food or service, it could be the people sitting next to me, or the atmosphere. It is time that I will never get back, so I want to enjoy it.

Everybody has a story. It's whether you choose to find some value in it.

If I go to a restaurant and the server is giving poor service, I ask him if he has five minutes to talk about what it going on. I had a server tell me she had lost her mother two days ago, and still had to come to work. That was her story. I took the time to hear it.

I call and talk to people who I don't know all the time. When I started out 10 years ago, people would hang up on me. At first I was upset, but then I realized that feeling was about me, and not about them. I had no idea what was going on in their lives, and their responses may have had nothing to do with me. Now I have some empathy for them. Something is going on in their world, and I can't help. It all begins with understanding the individual. It is not about me, it is about them.

171

I find that people are not afraid to change; they are afraid of change.

Times have changed; we are not the society we were 20 years ago. And times keep changing, and will continue to change. People understand that tomorrow will be different from today. But they are afraid of where they will be in 20 years. They are not afraid to change as an individual, but are afraid of change because of the unknown factor. I have four children. My oldest son is 22 and my youngest daughter is five. As a father, I am not afraid of my children getting older each day, because they are changing daily. Thinking where they will be years from now scares me. It has to do with the unknown.

172

I knew early on that I couldn't control everything. Nonetheless, the choices still exist—whether they are your choices or you are just reacting. There is always choice. You have the ability to steer your ship.

We are in constant evolution. It is important to reflect on the fact that change never stops. As change is happening, you have choices.

I Am

I am from John and Donna, who divorced when I was five years old.

I am a product developed from an early childhood through a motorcycle club lifestyle, where Death Before Dishonor existed, and corruption was everyday life.

I am from a mother who was married nine times, and a father who never left his committed lifestyle—I buried both my parents by the time I was 35.

I am carrying my school records with me because we moved so much, and the records would not make it before we were gone again.

I am a student who went to six different schools in one year, and still maintained above a "C" average during that year.

I am an individual who moved out on his own at age 16 in a state where no other relatives lived.

I am an example of change; I chose a life that resides in the minority of statistics, and not the majority.

I am a person who has never been to jail, or arrested for anything.

I am a father of four children who fill my life with joy every day.

I am a believer that living is not what you can accomplish for yourself, but what legacy you can leave behind to help others continue to grow.

MIKE CHATWOOD

{6}

DREAM YOUR OWN STORY

We invite you to discover your own unique way of moving through the world and how that informs your natural way of leading. When we share our stories and reflect on the experiences we've had, we gain the wisdom to evolve past our own limiting beliefs.

Create your **Story** and **I Am Poem**: think about where you come from, significant events that have influenced you, what you want out of life, and how you want to feel.

Communicate your Story and I Am Poem: share your story with someone, be open to questions and feedback.

Challenge yourself to grow: take a risk, confront your fear, and try something you haven't done before as a result of this process.

Collaborate with others: engage key people in your life, invite them to be part of your future story, and disconnect from those that don't support where you are going.

Elemental Interview Process

Find a witness to interview you using the attached format and record the conversation. Consider sharing two stories—one of personal change and one where you lead others through change. Complete the bolded questions for each story shared. At the end of your interview, title the conversation. This is intended to be a Socratic process, so deeply explore your assumptions, question viewpoints, and discuss implications and consequences of the events shared. The bulleted questions are optional and should be used sparingly to draw out specific details, context, etc. Create your story from the recordings.

Questions

Story 1: Tell me about your story of personal change. Describe the context, what happened, and why it was significant for you.

Story 2: Now tell me a story about when you influenced change in others. Describe the context, what happened, and why it was a significant for you.

1) Looking back on the story, what changes occurred as a result of your experience?
- What was the impact of those changes on you or others?
- What do you think drove the change?
- Explain how the change happened in steps?
- Did you initiate the change or were you reacting to the circumstances?
- Did you feel "in control" of the change?

2) Looking at things from a slightly different angle, what did not change?

- Describe what you expected versus what happened?
- If change occurred, but did not last, why do you think that was?
- Do you ever wonder what else could have happened?
- Were there opportunities lost?
- Have you continued to change and grow beyond your experiences in the story?

3) Why do you feel change happened?

- How did you feel as you were going through this experience?
- Why did you act or react to the events in the way that you did?

4) In retrospect is there anything you would change about your experience, or do differently?

- Did this experience change you, your behaviors, or your approach to life?
- Are there elements of change that have since reverted back to the way they were before the experience?

5) What was your single greatest takeaway from this experience.

In Closing

How would you title this conversation?

Write Your I Am Poem

Get creative by writing an "I Am" poem that begins with the statement, "I Am from…" You will be amazed at how quickly this allows you to convey what is important to you both past and present. This exercise should take no more than 15-20 minutes to complete. Here are some questions to consider as you write your poem:

1. What are your personal interests?

2. What are some highlights in your life?

3. What stimulates your passion?

4. Who surrounds you in life?

5. What is the most important lesson you have learned?

Create a Personal Vision

Creating a vision is a highly personal process with no right or wrong way of completing the process. That said, here are a few guidelines you may find helpful.

- **Give yourself plenty space and time to complete this process.** Remember there are no deadlines when it comes to your own happiness.
- **Commit to working on this when you are doing something you enjoy.** Make this project a reason to spend time relaxing, having fun, or being creative. It will help you connect with what you want more of in your day-to-day reality.
- **Consider the areas of your life that are important and include them in your vision** (e.g. family, work, finances, relationships, health, living space, etc.) Be creative in considering where you want to focus your attention and energy.
- **Create your vision from the perspective of how you want to feel.** This is not an exercise in goal setting, making resolutions, or expanding your to do list. This is about getting in touch with what makes you feel good and using that as a guide for the changes you want to make. So often we focus on outcomes without really understanding the underlying motivation. For example, is it money you want, the lifestyle it affords you, or a sense of freedom?

An example of a personal vision created using this process can be found in *How It All Works* under *Chris' Story.*

179

ABOUT THE AUTHOR

I am seen and loved beyond measure; blessed to be with my soul mate and surrounded by our six amazing kids.

I am from two loving parents whose example taught me what it means to show up in life.

I am someone who has to embody things to learn, often finding my solutions on the way to helping others.

I am happiest when I am in nature, traveling, teaching, or making an authentic connection.

I am learning to laugh more, to play more, and to give myself a break.

I am lucky to have so many in my life who challenge and inspire me each and every day.

I am still emerging.

Chris Richardson

ABOUT THE AUTHOR

I am happy living in the present, born of people I never met and headed toward a future I can only imagine.

I am privileged to be adopted by Homer and Rae, missionary linguists who dedicated 50 years to the translation of the Bible for native tribes around the world.

I am from 10 schools in 12 years constantly making new friends and facing new opportunities.

I am moving constantly having lived in 30 places by the time I was 30 and that instilled in me an extreme sense of adaptability and flexibility that has served me well.

I am blessed to have visited over 125 countries to date meeting so many wonderful people and experiencing so many diverse cultures.

I am a person who rejects all man-made religions having seen the horror their members perpetrate in the name of their God/gods all over the world.

I am in my own personal relationship with my Creator thanking him daily for all my life's blessings.

I am the result of many bad choices with many more good choices, some made by me and some made for me.

I am the product of experiencing the very worst and very best of man and feel I am such a better person as a result.

I am in a constant state of evolution incessantly curious, enthusiastically growing, always living passionately.

I am redefining myself to my best potential every moment of every day, ever a student of life.

I am all about connecting with other growers, helping them define success in life, and supporting their balanced pursuit of their visions.

I am all about my six amazing kids, watching them develop into incredible adults in spite of all my mistakes as a parent and giving them my unconditional love.

But most of all, I am all about the special moments with my soul mate when we are together being present and sharing in all our blessings.

Randall Gifford

ABOUT THE ILLUSTRATOR

I am listening to Wilco and wearing a Short Run Comix Festival tee.

I am typing near a friend's bulldog puppy who barks in his dreams.

I am drawing cartoons for a museum anniversary!

I am smitten by alleys of grass.

I am chewed gum blue and wondering about you.

Edie Everette

INDEX OF AUTHORS:

We are profoundly grateful and deeply honored to have collaborated with the following authors.

Made in the USA
Charleston, SC
22 May 2015